Tales of a 1960s Steam Traveller

44949 and 45110 pound up to Chapel with the Severn Valley Rail Tour
20 April 1968

Tales of a 1960s Steam Traveller

Ray Trader

ATHENA PRESS
LONDON

Tales of a 1960s Steam Traveller
Copyright © Ray Trader 2006
All photographs by the author

All Rights Reserved

No part of this book may be reproduced in any form
by photocopying or by any electronic or mechanical means,
including information storage and retrieval systems,
without permission in writing from both the copyright
owner and the publisher of this book.

ISBN 1 84401 637 4

First Published 2006 by
ATHENA PRESS
Queen's House, 2 Holly Road
Twickenham TW1 4EG
United Kingdom

Printed for Athena Press

*To my fellow enthusiasts from all over the country, for your friendship,
advice and assistance during those hectic last years.
We shared information, food and drink, the heat and the cold,
the joy and the pain – thanks to you all.*

Author's Note

I was born and raised in Salford, Lancashire, which meant that I had the unpredictable benefit of living amongst the last working steam locomotives on British Rail, but also made me slow to realise that the end was rapidly approaching.

The withdrawal of the Duchesses in September 1964 brought me to reality, and for the last three years (1965-68) I spent virtually all my non-working time searching for steam-hauled passenger trains – and this is my story.

Contents

The Summer of 1965	11
Lead-up to 18 April 1966	33
Summer of 1966	43
From Winter into Spring 1967	59
The Last Summer Saturday	73
The *Belfast Boat Express* (*BBE*)	79
The End of Manchester Steam	93
The End of Steam	111
The Very End of Steam	131

The Summer of 1965

By the spring of 1965 most of the local services in the north-west of England were operated by DMUs and many expresses were diesel-hauled, but there were still a large number of steam-worked passenger trains and it was possible to cover virtually every line behind steam at some time of the day or night. I had worked through the winter, saving as much money as possible so that I could take three months off during the summer to savour all the aspects of the remaining steam workings and those three months (but *not* the money) were to last for three years!

Let's go back to Manchester Victoria on the evening of Saturday, 1 May, where I'm relaxing in the first coach of the 2022 to Liverpool Exchange, headed by 70050 (5A), which is on a long Crewe North diagram having arrived on the 0810 from Windermere. We are just about to depart when Newton Heath 45600 rolls in with the stock of the 2105 to Heysham and, with hindsight (and practise), I should have jumped off and changed trains, for I was never to have a Jubilee on the *Belfast Boat*, but I stayed on the Liverpool as I needed the Britannia for haulage!

On Tuesday, 4 May I watched the morning peak arrivals at Victoria – 45055 (8M) 0700 from Southport (regular, returned on the 1710 Club), 45203 (9D) on the 0655 from Southport (DMU failure), 45343 (9D) 0755 Southport, 45246 (9D) 0725 Blackpool North, 42587 (8F) 0800 Orrell, 44933 (9D) 0756 Liverpool Exchange, 45093 (5B) 0700 Barrow and 70033 (5B) 0810 Windermere. Evening peak departures on the tenth were 44686 (8M) 1610 Southport, 42115 (9D) 1648 Horwich, 42295 (8F) 1714 Stockport Edgeley (all that remained of the through workings from Central Lancashire), 45202 (9D) 1703

The Summer of 1965

Blackpool North, 45055 (8M) 1710 Southport, and 45395 (6B-ex-works) on the 1722 Windermere.

Next day I went to Warrington Bank Quay, and Britannias were plentiful – 70044 on the 1100 Windermere to Crewe, 70051 1349 Crewe to Carlisle, 70020 1647 Crewe to Blackpool, 70028 1837 Crewe to Windermere plus 42948 (8F) arrived on the 1735 from Wigan but only one Scot, 46140 on a down freight. I returned on the 1630 from Holyhead with 45279 (6G) but missed the twelve-minute connection with the 2055 Heysham at Victoria.

About this time, I must have got the (mistaken) idea that the unrebuilt Bullied Pacifics were about to be withdrawn for, on 19 May, I made a hectic day trip to Southampton and back to try and travel behind one! Arriving at Waterloo, I noted 73110 on the 0930 to Bournemouth, but then decided on a quick dash to Southall where 7029 (*with* nameplates) was on shed and rostered for the 1615 Paddington to Banbury, so I now made this train my main target. However, on returning to Waterloo, 34041 was ready to leave on the 1330 to Weymouth so, reverting to Plan 'A', I went down to Southampton on this train. Here I noted 35023 on the *Belle* and 6853 on the York to Bournemouth before catching 76060 to Eastleigh and then returning to Waterloo behind 34064 on the 1828. I had succeeded in travelling with two unrebuilts but missed Clun and the 1615 (my last chance!)

The following day (the twentieth), the 1605 Victoria to Barrow was diverted via Hellifield due to a derailment and I travelled behind 44697 (9D) over the now rare Blackburn to Hellifield line, but the load was reduced from the usual nine coaches to only four as there was no Morecambe portion. At Carnforth I noted Fowler 42322 on the 1918 to Wennington.

On the twenty-fifth, the 1610 Central to Sheffield was worked by a B1 (61313) so I rode out to Romiley and then

The Summer of 1965

dashed back to Piccadilly, but I just missed another Fowler, 42327 (9G), leaving on the 1720 to Hayfield.

The first weekend of June was the traditional Whit holidays, and started in grand manner on the Friday (fourth) when a very clean 45654 (9B) arrived on the 0700 from Barrow, followed by 70010 (5A) with the 0810 Windermere. Later, 70016 left Victoria on the 1703 to Blackpool North and a relief to the 1700 Liverpool to Newcastle was hauled by 44767 (12A), followed by the main train, double-headed by 73160 (9H) and 44907 (8A)! Then 45182 (12C) arrived on the 1303 from Workington and the last remaining Metro-Vick diagram into Manchester had bitten the dust! On Saturday morning, 70016 worked the 0920 to Weymss Bay CTAC, 45600 (9D) the 0945 to Barrow and 70000 arrived on the Windermere.

I then headed for Scotland with a one-week rover and early on 9 June I left Carlisle on the down *Northern Irishman* behind 45018 (12A) – a tough job for a 'five' over the direct line via Newton Stewart.

I returned from Stranraer on the 0800 to Dumfries with 80117 (67E), then, after visiting Hurlford shed, I had 80091 (67B) to Ayr, where 45489 (67B) later arrived from St Enoch and 73101 (67A) worked the stock back as the 1915 departure to Glasgow – presumably a DMU working.

Next morning at Buchanan Street, 60007 (61B) arrived with the 0710 from Aberdeen and I headed north behind 73149 (65B), planning to return on the A4-rostered 1330 from Aberdeen, but 60034 failed at Perth to be replaced by 45115 on to Glasgow! The evening peak departures from Buchanan Street were a magnificent sight – 60007 on the 1730, 73147 (65B) 1735 to Callender, 45016 (65J) 1750 Callender and the grand finale – 60031 (65B) on the 1815 to Dundee.

Next day I planned to cover rare track on the 1442 Crail to Thornton Junction, but after visiting Dunfermline and

The Summer of 1965

Thornton sheds I only had time to reach Largo before returning on the 1442 behind 61343 (62A) with two coaches and a van. Next day I headed for Aberdeen and was rewarded with 60006 on the 1330 and I travelled right through to Glasgow – just in case – returning to Perth on the 1815 Dundee with 61147 (62B) – but where was 60031?

The thirteenth was a Sunday, so I decided on a mammoth shed bash, visiting Corkerhill, Polmadie (45531 and 60512 in steam but 60527/35 stored), St Pollox (60031 on shed!), Polmont (65243 Maude in steam with a buffer-beam snow-plough!) Dalry Road, St Margarets (60041 in steam, 60052 under repair) and Grangemouth (77006/9 on shed). I then headed south with 45236 (12A) on the 2328 Edinburgh to Manchester (to Carstairs) where 70036 arrived on the Glasgow portion and the combined train was taken on to Carlisle by the Pacific piloted by 45171 (64D). I returned north over the G&SW behind 70006 on the 0321 Carlisle to Kilmarnock (a good train for sleeping on) and then 45490 (67B) on the 0620 Kilmarnock to Glasgow via Dalry, (the Britannia followed on the 0720). I then crossed to Central and caught 80121 (66A) on the 0950 to Gourock, returning at 1055 with 76070 (66A). On the outskirts of Glasgow I was surprised (and delighted) to see an immaculate Royal Scot – 46115 – on freight.

My next objective was the Waverley line, but the only way I could be sure of steam haulage was on locals so I returned to Carlisle – noting 46140 on Polmadie and 72006 on the 1332 Carlisle to Perth. On arrival, 43040 was in the south bay, heading the 1805 to Appleby, but I made for the north bays where I boarded the 1813 to Hawick, headed by 61191 (64A). I sat back to enjoy the scenery and savour the atmosphere of a rural stopping train and, after Newcastleton, the B1 started the climb to Whitrope and, although only hauling three coaches, the crisp exhaust was a joy to hear. We stopped in the wilds of Riccarton Junction and, after a short silence, I could hear steam exhausts: looking north, I

The Summer of 1965

saw on the long curve 61029 and a V2 on a southbound car carrier, and they pounded through the station, accelerating from the summit. The stopper then completed the climb and dropped down into Hawick where, feeling tired, I decided to seek a bed and breakfast.

A porter directed me to turn left out of the station and walk up the hill. After about a quarter of a mile I saw a vacancy sign and, on knocking, a lady opened the door and, yes, she had a room for the night – at the back of the house. I soon fell asleep but was awakened in the middle of the night by a three-cylinder engine working hard. I jumped out of bed, looked out of the window and realised that the house overlooked the line – 60813 pounded past on freight, bright red rockets piercing the darkness! I then returned to bed and sleep but woke again just after dawn when I could hear more thrash. I opened the window and 60970 was storming up the 1 in 75, so near that I felt I could almost touch it – what a wonderful location to spend the night!

I then dressed, had breakfast, and headed for the shed – 76049, 78047 and 61396 there – and on to the station where the 0805 to Edinburgh was waiting, 80122 with four coaches. The morning was sunny, so I could enjoy the views and watch station activity on the journey and, all too soon, we arrived at Waverley and my unusual but enjoyable journey was over. This was the last day of my rover, so I made for Perth, hoping for an A4 on the 1330 from Aberdeen. My luck was in, as an immaculate 60009 rolled in and I rode through to Glasgow on what may have been my last A4 haulage. At Buchanan Street, 60019 headed the 1730 Aberdeen but I had to cross to St Enoch and caught 45490 on the 1825 to Kilmarnock, after which my next steam-ride was 73138 (9H) on the Manchester portion of the 2335 Glasgow from Wigan.

On Saturday, 19 June I spent the day at Chester, travelling out on the 0752 Exchange to Llandudno behind 45184 (6A). The highlight was between 1225 and 1305 when three Jubilees passed through (non-stop!) with Excursions to

The Summer of 1965

North Wales – 45600/04/32. Six Patricroft Caprottis – 73128/30/31/35/36/40 – and 24 black fives were on timetabled passenger workings. Only one GW loco passed through, 6921 (81E), light engine, presumably off a freight, and I returned home behind 45345 (6J) on the 1620 from Holyhead.

The following Friday (twenty-fifth), I was able to travel non-stop from Central to Liverpool Central with 42112 (9E) on a short-dated train from Sheffield Victoria which had been worked by 78007 (9E) from Guide Bridge.

Next day, I studied the summer Saturday workings at Exchange/Victoria and the notables were 70016 (12A) on the 1010 to Workington, 45562 (55C) arriving at 1226 on the Scarborough, and 70011 (12B) on the 1330 to Barrow. The 0900 to Filey was headed by 45436 (8B) banked by 82000(9H) and the 0950 Llandudno to Bradford left behind 45429 (6A), piloted by 46412 (9D). 44686 (8M) had a busy day, after presumably arriving earlier, working the 1258 to Southport, the 1850 return and finally heading for home on the 2100.

Most of the Rochdale to Liverpool locals were still steam and at Bolton on the twenty-ninth I noted 44686 (again!) on the 0735 Southport to Rochdale, 45385 (8F) on the following 0805, 46402 (8K) the 0840 Rochdale to Liverpool and 42183 (9K) on the 0950 to Liverpool. I returned to Manchester with 44773 (8A) on the 0700 Barrow which was followed by 70018 (5A) on the 0810 Windermere.

There was a shock on the thirtieth when the Windermere arrived behind a Type 4 (*ugh!*) but it was a one-off and 70027 (5A) headed the Barrow. I later had a numerical coincidence when I went to Bolton with 44890 (9D) on the Heysham and returned on the 2010 Blackpool North behind 44891 (9D).

The Summer of 1965

Into July, and the summer 1305 (FSO) Manchester/Liverpool to Glasgow began running on the second and I caught 45336 (9D) to Preston where immaculate 45721 (8K) had arrived with the Liverpool portion and then worked the combined train north. I sampled the Jubilee roar on a heavy train to Lancaster and, after watching *Impregnable* depart, I caught 41221 (10J) on the connecting Morecambe local. Back at Lancaster, 70010 (12A) flashed through on the 1530 (FO) Crewe to Glasgow before I returned to Preston behind 45390 (10A) on the Lakeside to Blackpool North return excursion where 70017 arrived on the 1837 Crewe to Windermere, to be replaced by 45092 (10A), and I returned home with 70003 (12A) on the 2010 Blackpool North to Manchester Victoria.

Next day (third), I travelled over Standedge to Leeds with 45056 (5B) on the 0930 (SO) Exchange to Newcastle and when 60154 (55H) took over I just had to sample the A1 to Harrogate! Back at Leeds, 61313 arrived on the 0914 from Llandudno before I returned with 45056 on the 1355 to Manchester.

The following Saturday (tenth) was Jubilee heaven – 45604 (9D) on the 1115 Victoria to Blackpool North, 45694 (8K) 1205 Blackpool North to Liverpool Exchange and 45627 (8K) returning with the 1400 Glasgow plus 70001 (12A) on the up Lakes, 70017 1220 Blackpool to Euston, 70013 Dundee to Blackpool and 70018 (5B) on the 1648 Crewe to Blackpool South.

The previous week, 45705 had been transferred to Trafford Park and on the thirteenth it was rostered for the 1722 to Buxton. I arrived at Central just after 5 p.m. but not only was there no Jubilee in sight, there was no train either.

Due to flooding at Chorlton, the Buxton was starting from Oxford Road! I dashed along but *Seahorse* was already crossing the road bridge on its way toward Piccadilly – I had just missed a unique journey! The following evening I arrived

The Summer of 1965

early at Central and the 1722 was in its usual place (Platform Six) with 45705 in charge of the four-coach formation. I had time to take several photographs before claiming a window seat in the first coach to enjoy the climb to Peak Forest and on to Buxton. At Chinley, the connecting 1832 to Sheffield via the Hope Valley was headed by 61093.

The following Saturday (seventeenth), I spent the morning at Victoria – 45062 (9J) on the 0900 Exchange to Filey, 70010 on the 1010 to Workington, 70020 arrived on the 0700 Barrow and 45430 (2J!) passed through with the Bradford to Llandudno. The reverse working did stop at Victoria so I boarded and travelled over the Calder Valley line to Bradford behind 44693 (56D). I then caught 42161 (56A) on the 1508 to Wakefield (TC to KX) and returned with Fowler 42406 (56A) on the 1636 back. Passing Ardsley shed, 60923 was in steam but 60133 was stored.

The next day (Sunday, 18 July), I purchased a six-day Northern Runabout ticket and, on reflection, this not only marked the beginning of my almost continuous steam travelling, but also was when I begin to meet fellow enthusiasts from all parts of the country who were to so enrich my life. I spent the Sunday on a relaxed trip to Llandudno – out with 73160 (9H) on the 0935 from Exchange, returning behind 73136 (9H) on the 1309.

Notable on Junction shed (6G) were 45562 (55C) and 70000 (5B). In the evening, I travelled out to Wigan Wallgate for 75048 (8K) on the 1734 Liverpool Exchange to Rochdale and the 2037 return – the only Sunday steam working on the route. Next day I aimed for the Lakeside branch beginning with 42436 (10D) on the 0916 Wigan (NW) to Preston, where I joined the 1047 Blackpool to Lakeside headed by 45328 (10A). I alighted at Ulverston and fitted in a trip to Barrow shed before returning to Ulverston for 46433 (10J) on the 1555 to Lakeside where the Ivatt ran round and then formed the 1655 to Morecambe. Later, at

Carnforth, 42322 (10A) worked the 1916 to Wennington, 45294 (12C) was on the 1722 Manchester to Windermere and on shed were 45530 (0530 freight to Carlisle) and 45698 8K (0435 to Liverpool). At Preston, 70018 headed the 2029 Blackpool South to Crewe before I returned to Manchester with 44696(9B) on the 2010 Blackpool North. On Tuesday, the West Coast trains were being diverted via St Helens (due to a derailment) and after catching 42574 (9K) on the 0950 from Bolton through to Liverpool Exchange and returning to Wigan behind 42174 (8F) on the 1140 return, I crossed to North Western and picked up the 1100 Windermere down to Warrington via St Helens and Earlestown.

The loco was the rare 45027 which had just been transferred to Carnforth from Bletchley. Back to Victoria and 70012 (5A) was on the 1607 Barrow but I chose 44686 (8M) with the 1610 Southport – maybe I thought that the variants would soon be withdrawn. Later, I joined Agecroft's 45424 on the obscure 1710 from Clifton Junction to Liverpool then 75047 (8F) on the 1940 to Preston where 70028 (5A) arrived on the 2029 Blackpool South but was unable to continue to Crewe due to a failure, so I returned home behind 45291 (9B) on the 2010 Blackpool North. This train departed from Platform Two and as we left I looked across to the L and Y side – 45721 was on the 2145 to Liverpool!

The Horwich branch was due for closure, so next morning (21 July) I caught the 0750 from Chorley, a push-and-pull working, with 84025 (9K), then back to Bolton on the 0811 from Horwich worked by 42626 (9K). I then had 46402 (8K) on the 0917 Bolton to Liverpool Exchange 45440 (8A) up to Preston at 1105, 44934 (9D) into Blackpool and back to Preston for the down *Lakes Express*, headed by 45109 (8B), to Oxenholme where 42613 (10A) was waiting with the 1730 to Windermere. After a pleasant stroll to the lake, I returned south at 2030 with 70018 (5B), which had arrived on the 1722 from Manchester.

The Summer of 1965

So to Friday, the last day of my rover, and my target had to be the 1310 Liverpool to Glasgow hoping for a Bank Hall Jubilee. As I had all morning to reach Liverpool I took a devious route – 0840 Rochdale to Wigan (46402), over to North Western for the 0620 Carlisle to Crewe (45081 (12B) with self-weighing tender) down to Warrington, 73011 (9H) to Chester (1005 Manchester to Holyhead) and 42252 (6A) 1122 Chester to Rock Ferry. Across the Mersey, on to Exchange and the long walk up the platform and I was fortunate – a clean 45698 was preparing to depart. At Preston the Manchester portion arrived behind 44934 (9D) and Mars had to summon all his strength to get the combined eleven-coach load underway. On the approach to Oxenholme we halted and 42210 (1215) was attached as pilot through to Shap Summit but, despite the two stops, we arrived in Carlisle only one minute late.

45013 (12A) left on the 1637 to Bradford, 76050 (64G) headed to 1813 to Hawick, 70054 (5A) worked the 1530 (FO) Crewe to Glasgow throughout and 70033 departed on the 2027 to Perth, but I decided to book into a nearby bed and breakfast for the night and spend all day Saturday on Carlisle station studying the steam passenger workings – and here's what I saw (24 July 1965):

76049	64G	arrive 0630	Hawick
43049	12A	arrive 0800	Appleby
44672	12A	depart 0900	Glasgow (St Enoch)
44731	8B	arrive 0600	Warrington
44937	12B	arrive (1015)	Morecambe – Glasgow
73103	67A	depart (1010)	Newcastle – Stranraer
45297	5B	depart (1045)	Newcastle – Blackpool
44724	67C	arrive (1037)	Heads of Ayr
44677	12A	depart 0835	Glasgow – Leeds
45425	8F	0920	Southport – Glasgow
44906	8A	arrive	Blackpool – Glasgow
45138	12A	depart	Blackpool – Glasgow

The Summer of 1965

60131	55H	depart 1239	to Leeds (arrived 0225?)
45684	8K	arrive 0930	Liverpool – Glasgow
44883	12A	depart 0930	Liverpool – Glasgow
44948	10A	depart	Blackpool – Glasgow Relief
45626	55A	arrive 0930	Leeds – Glasgow Rel
45120	12A	depart 0930	Leeds – Glasgow Rel
70054	5A	arrive	Glasgow – Blackpool N
44680	5B	depart (1315)	Glasgow – Blackpool N
45675	55A	1015	Leeds – Glasgow (through)
70003	12A	depart 1332	Aberdeen
45593	55A	arrive (1336)	CTAC (Leeds)
45029	66B	depart	CTAC (Leeds)
70033	12A	arrive (1408)	Dundee – Blackpool N
45481	12A	arrive 1208	From Hellifield
45385	8F	depart (1606)	Glasgow – Morecambe
45013	12A	depart	Glasgow Relief
45307	8A	arrive	Blackpool – Dundee
45126	12A	depart	Blackpool – Dundee
70031	5B	depart	Relief to Glasgow (Via G&SW)
70019	5A	arrive	Glasgow – Morecambe
45254	12A	depart 1637	to Bradford
73099	66A	arrive	CTAC (to Leeds)
45626	55A	depart	CTAC (to Leeds)
45698	8K	1400	Through Glasgow – Liverpool
45660	55A	(1638)	Through St Pancras – Glasgow
70005	12A	arrive	Stranraer – Newcastle
44790	12A	arrive 1540	From Bradford
45018	12A	(ex-works)	through 1612 Crewe – Glasgow

Next day (Sunday), I went over to the north-east on a shed-bash and the highlight (or lowlight) was at Tyne Dock, where A1s 60116/27/32/42 looked magnificent but were actually stored and condemned.

The Summer of 1965

On returning to Carlisle I purchased a second Scottish Rover and early on the Monday morning I watched 70005 (12A) take over the down *Northern Irishman* but the train was wedged and, feeling exhausted, I waited for the following 0321 to Ayr headed by 70008. The Britannia came off at Kilmarnock (to work the 0720 to St Enoch) and 80091 (67B) took the 0321 forward and I stayed on, eventually reaching Glasgow behind 45432 (67E) on the 0610 from Annan.

After a fill-in turn to Gourock (42265 out and 73099 back), I crossed to Buchanon Street, and caught 45084 (65J) to Stirling on the 1300, returning behind 45214 (65J) on the 1415. I didn't have long to wait, for an A4-60019 (61B) was heading the 1625 to Perth so I climbed aboard and savoured the power of the Pacific (unfortunately I have lost all my logs for this period). At Perth, 73152 (65B) was on the next Glasgow but I waited for the 1730 from Buchanon Street and my luck held; 60009 (61B) was at its head and I was soon on my way to Aberdeen in style.

Early next morning I caught the 0710 to Glasgow with 60009 down to Stirling and then headed for Carlisle for the 1332 back to Perth, powered by 70009 (12A). The 1625 from Glasgow was a five (44997 – 63A) and the 1710 to Aberdeen had another (44794 – 61B) so I returned south behind 70041 (12A) on the 2025. The Brit came off at Carstairs but I stayed on to sleep to Carlisle where 70039 (12A) arrived on the up *Northern Irishman* and 70001 (12a) took over the down working to Stranraer. A fellow enthusiast informed me of an 1826 Edinburgh to Dundee relief-booked steam so after spending the morning on Glasgow locals and then 45011 (66E) on the 1320 Edinburgh to Lanark, I returned to Waverley with 45138 (12A) on the 1510 from Carstairs. I had time to fit in the Corstorphine branch with 80122 (64A) on the 1718 before catching the relief, headed by 60973 (62B), through to Dundee.

As we arrived, 60836 (62B) was pounding south on

The Summer of 1965

freight, immediately followed by 60027 (64A) on a through freight. I walked to the shed and 60530/32 were spare so I decided to find a bed and breakfast for the night. Next morning 60530 had gone (had I missed something?) but 60528 had arrived, so I caught the 1000 to Glasgow headed by 73154 (65B). After the usual Gourock trip, I returned to Buchanon Street for the 1625 again headed by a five (44705 – 63A), and at Stirling I noticed 61278 (62B) tender-first on the 1724 to Callender so I changed trains to sample this unusual working. On arrival, the B1 ran round and formed the 1810 to Edinburgh and I travelled through to Waverley. I then had 45029 (66B) on the 2105 to Carstairs, where I joined the 2027 Carlisle to Perth, hauled by 70039 (12A). I alighted at Stirling and my choice was either a bed and breakfast or an overnight to Aberdeen and, feeling fresh, I had a meal and returned to the station.

My luck was in, for 60009 headed the 2300 from Glasgow and I joined other enthusiasts in the first coach for the journey to Aberdeen. On arrival, we walked down to the docks and an all-night café where I learnt of an additional working at 1945 to Edinburgh rostered for an A4, so I planned the day with this in mind. We returned to the station and boarded the 0710 stock for a sleep, and I was woken by an engine backing on – 60019. I travelled to Stirling with Bittern and then down to Carlisle, returning on the 1332 worked by 70002 (12A). At Dunblane we crossed 60007 on the 1330 from Aberdeen, and then from Perth I had 44703 on the 1710 to Aberdeen. At Forfar, we crossed 60024 on the 1730 up – were there any A4s left to work the extra? Amazingly yes, for old faithful 60009 was coming off Ferryhill and duly worked the 1945 through to Waverley. I then caught the 2330 to Manchester (44726 – 12A) with 45013 (12A) working the following 2345 to Birmingham. At Carlisle, the main topic of conversation was that Scot 46115 had worked down to Liverpool on the FO 1400 from Glasgow and should return on today's 1310! I caught the 0321 to Ayr with 44972 (67B) to Kilmarnock and 80091 on to Ayr

23

The Summer of 1965

where the 0715 to Heads of Ayr was waiting – double-headed by a black five (44974 – 67C) and a standard Caprotti five, surely one of the St Rollox allocation but unbelievably it was Patricrofts 73134, ex-Cowlairs Works and 'borrowed' by Ayr shed! At the Heads of Ayr both engines ran round and formed the 0800 to Newcastle, and I travelled with the locos to Dumfries where 44974 uncoupled and I watched 73134 head south – would it get back to Manchester before I did? I crossed to the down side and returned north on the 1010 Carlisle to Stranraer, which arrived behind 45161 (67e) and was then piloted from Dumfries by 44974. I got off at Ayr and returned to Kilmarnock with 76098 and waited there for the 1325 St Enoch to Morecambe. As the train approached, my first impression was that the loco was a Britannia but as it got closer I realised that it was a Clan – 72007 (12A)! I jumped aboard and travelled to Carlisle where the Clan was replaced by 45212 (10A). I then waited for the 1310 Liverpool but the first arrival was 70018 on the 1305 Manchester to Glasgow, then 70045 on the 1638 to Glasgow St Enoch (relief *Thames-Clyde*) and, temptingly, 45698 (8K) returning home on the 1400 Glasgow, but where was *Scots Guardsman*? Finally, the Scot rolled in, late but still looking formidable, and thankfully working through to Glasgow.

I joined the crowded first coach and we all savoured the climb to Beattock and the descent to the Clyde valley and I was pleased that I had waited, for this was to be my last run behind a Royal Scot.

I then had a few days' recuperation at home until 4 August when I went to Victoria for the evening peak but caught the first departure as 70025 (5B) was on the 1607 to Barrow and as we passed Exchange the 1630 Llandudno was unusually headed by another Brit (70042). At Preston, 42374 (8F) arrived on the 1729 from Wigan (returning at 1910), 45563 (8B) powered the 1722 Manchester to Windermere, 45684 (8K) the 1939 Blackpool North to Liverpool and 70027 (5B) the 1648 Crewe to Blackpool South before I returned with

44861 (just transferred to 9D from Derby) on the 2010 from Blackpool and at Skew Bridge we passed 45531 (12A) heading north on freight.

From the tenth I began a week-long North-West Rover and on the first day I travelled over Ais Gill in leisurely style on locals, just enjoying the scenery and station activity. I travelled north with 45118 (12A) on the 1208 Hellifield to Carlisle and returned at 1637 to Skipton behind 44802 (12A) and at Kirby Stephen we crossed 70005(12A) on the 1540 from Bradford. Next day I planned to cover the down Lakes so after a morning trip to Ulverston on the 1047 Preston with 45095 (10A) and returning on the 1425 from Morecambe behind 44918 (8F) I caught the Lakes from Preston to Penrith with 44958 (10D) and then enjoyed the scenic Keswick line with 46432 (12D) to Workington where I visited the shed – 13 4F 0-6-0s in steam – before heading for Carlisle, hoping for the unexpected. There it certainly was – the 2125 Glasgow to St Pancras sleepers was double-headed by 73122/4 but unfortunately the first stop, Leeds, was beyond the validity of my rover! 70001 (12A) took over the down *Northern Irishman* and 70039 (12A) arrived with the up working – also 72008 (12A) was working the 0006 parcels to Glasgow. I headed south to Carnforth for the 0144 from Crewe, which arrived behind 44862 (officially 1A but probably on the way to 12A, which was replaced by 70012 (5B) to Barrow. I joined the train and slept most of the way to Whitehaven, then on to Workington for the up *Lakes Express*. 46432 (12D) was again in charge to Penrith where 42154 (10A) took over to Oxenholme where 70032 (12B) was waiting with the Windermere portion and the Pacific then worked the combined train on to Crewe.

Here, I took a few hours break and returned to the station in the late evening when 7812 (6D) arrived on the Shrewsbury to York mails. I headed north on the 0144 with 44833 (5B) to Carnforth and 45297 on to Barrow, returning on the 0630 with 44894 (10A) to Lancaster. I then headed for Windermere on the 0815 from Preston with 44684 (5B –

The Summer of 1965

third one that morning) and we soon crossed 70054 (5A) with the 0810 Windermere to Manchester and, while standing at Oxenholme, 46115 rolled through on an up freight. I returned at 1043 behind 44684 and on the approach to Oxenholme I had a grandstand view of 45531 (12A) storming north on freight before we picked up the Keswick portion (regular 42154). At Preston, 45039 (8A) headed north on the last Pilling Pig and 45627 (8K) arrived with the Liverpool to Blackpool. I turned this Jubilee down, gambling on the 1310 (FO) Liverpool to Glasgow, and I was rewarded when 45698 (8K) appeared, picked up the Manchester portion (44803-9D) and then worked the combined train forward. Mars must have been in fine condition, for the driver stormed both Grayrigg and Shap unassisted, but I decided to alight at Penrith for the 1400 (FO) return – wrong decision. It was diesel, so I had to suffer to Preston where 44803 (9D) took me home on the Manchester portion.

Next day (Saturday 14), I headed for the Settle and Carlisle line and reached Skipton in time for the 1015 Leeds to Glasgow – unusually powered by 70039 (12A) and I travelled over Ais Gill behind the Britannia to Appleby where I alighted, changed platform and waited for the 1239 Carlisle to Leeds. The near silence was broken by 45574 (55A) heading north on the CTAC from Leeds before 45608 (55A) arrived on the 1239 – at least I got one Jubilee over the wonderful route. At Hellifield, I bade farewell to *Gibraltar* and caught 44948 (10A) on the 1352 Leeds to Carnforth, joining the Morecambe portion which was worked by 42616 (10A) from Wennington. I then reached Carnforth in time for 45698 returning south on the 1400 (SO) Glasgow, and at Preston I joined the Manchester portion headed by 73128 (9H), unusual on a Newton Heath diagram.

The following week several Britannias were reallocated from Crewe to Newton Heath and on the seventeenth 70034 appeared on the 2055 Heysham and on the eighteenth and

The Summer of 1965

nineteenth 70024 worked the 1010 Victoria to Blackpool North and the 1912 return. Over at Central, 45705 was regularly working the 1722 Buxton and on the twentieth 45647 (55C) unexpectedly powered the 1845 Leeds to Liverpool.

The summer timetable was drawing to a close, so next day (Saturday 21) I headed for Birmingham Snow Hill to sample some Great Western motive power. I travelled down on a Bournemouth train which at Wolverhampton (LL) was taken over by 6952 (2D), and then returned on the northbound working with 7912 (2D). The following Eastbourne arrived behind 6917 (2D) and I then caught 7827 (6D) down to Snow Hill on a Bournemouth train, returning north with 4920 (82E) on a Portsmouth, followed by 6956 (81F) from Weymouth and 6924 (81F) on another Portsmouth. I then heard that 7029 was working the last train from Bristol, but as this would mean a long overnight I chickened out and headed for home.

The following Saturday (twenty-eighth), I went overnight to the North East, catching the Swansea to York Mails at Stockport powered by 45225 (9B) and 44943 (55C) to Leeds where 60118 (55H) took over to York and I returned with the A1 on the 0435 back to Leeds. Here there was an agonising choice – 45626 (55A) on the 0830 to Morecambe, 45581 (55C) on the 0908 Poole, or 60134 (55H) on the 0845 to York. I chose *Foxhunter*, and returned to Leeds where 70040 (12A) headed the 1015 to Glasgow, but 60118 had returned from Neville Hill and was waiting to take over the 0930 Manchester to Newcastle! The train arrived behind 73158 (9H) and when the A1 backed on there was a mass invasion of the first coach. I travelled all the way to Newcastle (even though it meant diesel back) and near Darlington we passed 60004 (61B) running in light engine after overhaul. I eventually reached Sheffield Midland in time for *Bihar and Orissa* on its return with the Poole and rode with the Jubilee over the rare route via Penistone to Huddersfield. I watched the

The Summer of 1965

Jubilee leave for Leeds and returned home tired, but savouring a wonderful day's travelling.

The beginning of September was the start of the football season and on the first, Manchester United had a midweek home fixture. There was a special service from Central to the Old Trafford platform and the outward workings commenced at 6 p.m. This was an awkward time for Trafford Park as their tanks and black fives had not returned from evening peak workings, so the only available motive power was – Stainer 8Fs! I caught the 1805 behind 48178 (9E) and the following 1833 was worked by 48356 (9E). The ECSs were taken back to Central by 45233 (9E) and 42455(9E) for the next departures, so the 8Fs retired to the shed after their brief spell of passenger work.

The weekend of 3/4 September was the last of the summer timetable and there were numerous options. The first had to be the 1310 (F0) Liverpool to Glasgow, so I started out on the 1010 Manchester Victoria to Blackpool North with 44697 (9D) as far as Preston, then 44817 (9J) on the 1152 to Liverpool Exchange, where I was greeted by the wonderful sight of immaculate 45721 (8K) ready to leave on the Glasgow. I eagerly climbed aboard and as we passed Bank Hall I caught a glimpse of 45684 in steam. At Preston the Manchester portion arrived behind 45271 (9D) and after this had been added, *Impregnable* roared away with his heavy load to Lancaster. There, the Jubilee stood in glorious sunlight as it took water and I used half a roll of film taking photographs from all angles, and a lovely going-away shot as it departed, but, tragically, light got onto the film (either in loading or developing) – the only time this ever happened to any of the many rolls I took during the Sixties – and *Impregnable* was withdrawn at the end of the month!

I returned home for a few hours' sleep before heading out to Huddersfield for the overnight York Mails, which arrived

The Summer of 1965

with the powerful combination of 45647 (55C) and 70015 (9B) – the 2200 Bradford connection had already arrived with 42108. The Jubilee/Brit combination pounded up to Standedge and at Stalybridge *Sturdee* came off to work the Manchester portion while I continued with *Apollo* to Stockport where an electric took over to Crewe. Here, 70052 (5B) left on the 0144 Barrow sleepers and 45407 (8C – ex-works) headed the Mails to Shrewsbury where 75063 (6D) was waiting to work the train on to Aberystwyth (drat – no Manor!). At Machynlleth I stumbled out into the morning air and then had to endure a DMU all the way to Pwllheli in order to catch the return through workings on their last day of running. After a walk to a local café, I returned to Pwllheli station for the 1030 to London headed by 75021 (6C), which I caught to Criccieth, where I waited for the following 1055 to Birmingham Snow Hill with 75013 (6F).

After enjoying the coastline scenery we turned inland and were piloted by 75014 (6D) up Talerddig and then crossed the down *Cambrian* which was Manor-powered by 7828. At Shrewsbury, 73036 (6D) took over to Snow Hill where I finally managed to be hauled by a GW loco, Grange 6849, back to Wolverhampton (LL) on a returning relief, before heading home.

By this time Southport shed had acquired a variety of Caprotti black fives and on the morning of the eighth I travelled to Wigan Wallgate on the 0718 from Bolton (44893 – 9K), from where I returned with 44757 (8M) on the 0735 Southport to Rochdale as far as Bolton and then the following 0805 with 44686 (8M) on to Rochdale. The next weekend I travelled on the York Mails in the opposite direction, starting at Shrewsbury with 44963 (8B) at 2250 to Crewe, then 70039 (12A) from Stockport to Leeds and finally 60154 (55H) on to York. After an early morning shed bash (60129/45/51 in steam) I returned to Leeds with *Foxhunter* on the 0435, then 42622 (55A) to Bradford (Forster Square) at

The Summer of 1965

0552, (77001/12 station pilots) and returned to City behind 43039 (55A) on the 0702. Leeds had a choice of Jubilees – 45643 and 45697 on specials and 45694 (56A) on a Blackpool *Parspec* via Copy Pit! I joined *Bellerophon* and at Sowerby Bridge very clean 45565 (56F) was waiting with a portion from Bradford and *Victoria* then headed the combined train through to Blackpool. We threaded the Calder Valley in morning sunshine and then stopped on Hall Royal Junction curve to acquire 48348 (10F) as a banker for the slog up to the summit. On the approach to Preston we were slowed by a distant 'on' and I stood by a door ready to detrain if we stopped but the signal changed to green and the Jubilee opened up through the platform and roared round the curve past the remains of the shed.

At Blackpool North we arrived at an excursion platform and much time (and film) was spent admiring *Victoria* before we were able to change platforms and return to Preston with 42431 (10C) on the two-coach 1650.

The weekend of 24/25 September brought the closure of the Horwich and Barnoldswick branches, so I began on the Friday with 42087 (9D) on the last 1648 Victoria to Horwich, returning with 84025 (9K) on the 1759 to Chorley – the final push-pull working. I then set out overnight on the York Mails behind 70015 (9B) from Stockport to Leeds where 60154 (55H) took over, but I had to refuse the A1 and make for Barnoldswick with 42072 (55F) on the 0400 Leeds to Bradford and then 42145 (55A) with the 0432 Shipley to Skipton, which would be the branch engine but, unfortunately, we had to bus it to Barnoldswick where 42145 was waiting to work the 0819 to Skipton. Despite rain, there were a fair number of locals to see the departure and, after taking a valedictory photograph, I climbed aboard for my last ride over the line. At Skipton, 84015 (10G) arrived with the obscure 0712 from Garsdale before I trekked across Lancashire by DMU to reach Horwich in time for the last

The Summer of 1965

departure at 1205, worked by 42626 (9K). Despite heavy rain, the tank looked smart with a farewell head-board and, after more photos, we climbed aboard for the last ride to Bolton and the summer of 1965 had really ended.

42626 at Horwich (last departure, 25 September 1965).

Lead-up to 18 April 1966

As the end of 1965 approached, the list of impending closures and withdrawals seemed almost endless – the S&D, IOW, GC AIs and all GW steam, so on Saturday, 18 December I set out overnight from Manchester on a circular route, travelling south on the S&D and returning along the GC and I also had an unexpected bonus in between.

I reached Bath Green Park in time for the 0648 to Bournemouth headed by 76013 (70F), travelling to Evercreech Junction where I changed to the 0815 to Highbridge and then the 0945 return, both worked by 41223 (83G). Back at Evercreech Junction, I joined the 0900 Bristol to Bournemouth with 80037 (83G) in charge and at Templecombe the train was pulled back on to the through line by 80043 (83G). On arrival at Bournemouth, 35030 was a fine sight on the 1030 Waterloo to Weymouth but I had to head the other way behind 76006 (70D) on the 1351 to Southampton. At Brockenhurst, 41224 (70F) had arrived on the connecting 1420 from Lymington but I travelled on to Southampton where I planned to wait for the following 1434 from Bournemouth to Waterloo, which duly arrived behind 35008 (70F) but I had been informed that the Plymouth to Brighton was steam-hauled and, as I had never even travelled the south coast line, I decided to wait. The 1330 from Waterloo was worked by 34005 (70S) before the Brighton arrived behind 34038 (70A) and I eagerly joined the train. The light was fading as I enjoyed the sound of a Bullied Pacific and the sight of stations like Fareham and Chichester which had previously been just names on a map to me and darkness had fallen by the time we reached Brighton. I took a long, last look at *Lynton* before catching an express to London – which conveniently stopped at Preston Park! From Victoria I crossed to Marylebone for the 2245 to Manchester

Lead-up to 18 April 1966

which was hauled by 70046 (2D) to Leicester, after which I fell into a much-needed sleep.

On Boxing Day I visited Newton Heath and was saddened by the sight of 45600 and 45632 on the scrap line (leaving only 45654 active here) and thoughts came flooding back of my footplate ride on *Bermuda* in the summer of 1961 during its many years at Patricroft.

New Year's Eve brought an agonising decision – do I go to Oxford for the last Western Region steam working, or to York for the last A1? I had to choose the latter and began my journey at Pendleton (Old) to catch the 0756 stopper from Liverpool Exchange into Victoria. I had travelled on this train many times over the years but this was to be my last, and it was fittingly headed by a local stalwart – Newton Heaths 44890. At Victoria, I watched the morning arrivals – the 0700 from Barrow (45076 – 9D), the 0810 from Windermere with ex-works 70054 (2D!) and the 0740 from Llandudno headed by regular 45282 (kept very clean by 6G). I then watched 44687 (8M) depart with the 1030 to Southport before heading to the Silver Pool for a hefty three-course lunch to sustain me through the long day and night ahead.

Well nourished, I walked over to Central to meet a friend and we boarded the 1345 to Sheffield (Midland) via the Hope Valley, behind 44888 (9E). This was an enjoyable journey on a pleasant winter afternoon – lovely scenery and pleasant chat about the past and the future, but from Sheffield we had to endure diesel-power to York where we were greeted by a magnificent sight – immaculate 60145 at the head of the 1830 relief to Newcastle. We joined the well-filled front coach for the journey north and on arrival at Newcastle many of the local enthusiasts got off but we stayed on board for the train returned as the 2030 back to York. From Darlington, with seven on (270 tons), *Saint Mungo* accelerated rapidly and reached 99 mph on level track at Tollerton before a signal

Lead-up to 18 April 1966

check and then signal stop outside York! The A1 covered forty-three and a half miles in 38 minutes 45 seconds and this was the nearest I ever came to a ton with steam!

Early on Saturday, 15 January, I set out on my regular overnight diagram beginning at Exchange with 73039 (9H) on the 0100 Glasgow to Wigan, then 44832 (5B) heading the 0144 Crewe to Barrow as far as Carnforth where 70027 (5B) took over, replaced at Barrow by 45372 (8F) on to Whitehaven. After a DMU to Workington (and feeling hungry), we asked a porter where we could get a hot breakfast and he replied 'in the staff canteen', and when we naively enquired how we got to it he pointed to a gap in the fence, saying, 'Through there!' We returned to the platform for the 1053 to Euston, headed by 45105 (12A), and the very friendly crew invited us on to the footplate! This was truly an invigorating experience – a sunny, clear morning, a very interesting line with rugged scenery. We remained on the engine until Askam (the last stop before Barrow) – what wonderful railwaymen in this far corner of England.

There was still a substantial amount of peak-hour steam at Manchester Central and a typical morning was on 27 January, when the first arrival was 43047 (9F) on the 0802 from Cheadle Heath followed by 43048 (9F) on the 0818. Then came four consecutive arrivals of the Liverpool line – 45188 (8c) on the 0712, 42697 (9E) on the 0730, 42287 (9E) on the 0819 from Irlam and 42583 (9E) the 0807 from Warrington. The next arrival was 45231 (6A) with the 0721 Chester Northgate which was rostered DMU, but regularly steam-worked right through till early 1967 and, finally, 44888 (9E) on the 0800 from Buxton (unfortunately *Seahorse* had made its last appearance in November 1965). The evening departures on 8/9 February began at 1712 with two departures – 42583 (9E) to Liverpool and 43048 (9F) to Cheadle Heath, then 44895 (9E) on the 1722 Buxton, 42076 (9E) the 1733 to Irlam, 42455 (9E) 1745 to Warrington and finally 43048's second trip at 1805.

Lead-up to 18 April 1966

I now planned a last visit to the Isle of Wight and, late on Friday, 11 February, I travelled south via Birmingham, fitting in a visit to Oxley where 6831/33/71 were still stored – the last Granges I ever saw. I eventually reached Bath Green Park for the 0647 to Bournemouth headed by 76013 (70F), and travelled all the way to Branksome, then had 34024 (70F) on the 1106 to Waterloo as far as Brockenhurst, where I joined the Lymington connection with 80032 (70F) down to the pier.

After crossing the water and then a bus ride to Cowes, I caught W35 on the 1431 to Ryde Esplanade and then had W22 on the 1528 to Ventnor and the 1642 return, before bidding farewell to this unique service and heading for Portsmouth. I travelled electric to Woking where I waited for the first steam to Waterloo, the 1550 from Weymouth powered by 34023 (70D). After waiting for the 2051 arrival (34012) and watching 34018 depart on the 2120 to Poole, I crossed to Marylebone for the 2245 to Manchester, worked by 44661 to Leicester, and eventually arrived home early on Sunday morning.

On 24 February, I watched the evening departures from Victoria – 45255 (9D) on the 1605 to Southport, 44874 (10A) 1607 Barrow, 45091 (8F) 1710 Southport, 44845 (9D) 1715 Blackpool South (normally DMU), 44905 (10A) 1722 Windermere and 44842 (8F) 1740 Southport, before travelling out to Wigan behind 45281 (8F) on the 1810 Southport. I returned to Manchester with 45255 on its next working (1900 Southport) and at Victoria there was the unexpected sight of a B1 – 61255 (50B) – on the 2022 stopper to Liverpool Exchange, so I climbed aboard for a second trip to Wigan!

I again went overnight on the twenty-seventh, starting out on the 2220 Exchange to Holyhead behind 45042 (6B) to Warrington; then the 0144 Crewe with ex-works 45421 (10D from 10C – Fleetwood had just closed) to Carnforth and 70027 (5B) on to Barrow. I returned on the 0630 with 44709

Lead-up to 18 April 1966

(10A) changing at Carnforth on to the following 0700 to Manchester headed by 44778 (10A). I alighted at Lancaster to watch the action – 46486 (10J) had arrived with the three-coach Morecambe portion of the 0700, 70028 (5B) worked the 0815 Preston to Windermere and I then headed south behind 70025 (5B) on the 0810 from Windermere and I took the opportunity to travel through to Manchester. I returned north on the 1115 Victoria to Blackpool North but after taking 20 minutes to reach Bolton the driver failed the engine (45336-9D) and the local shed sent out a replacement which, at the time, seemed just another black five, but it was 45110 (9K) – the only time that I was hauled by this now famous loco in BR days! I stayed on to Preston then had 44733 (10A) on the 1235 to Windermere, 44681 (5B) on the 1425 Morecambe to Crewe, 70054 (12a) on the 1349 Crewe to Carlisle, 70035 (12A) the 1550 Lancaster to Barrow, before returning home behind 45326 (10A) on the 1303 from Workington to Manchester.

Next day (twenty-seventh), 90456 (36C) was an unusual visitor on Patricroft and 73125/29/34/43 were stored.

On 3 March, I made a round trip to Carlisle starting on the 0100 with 73035 (9M) to Wigan, where I waited for the 0144 in the famous (or infamous?) down side waiting-room. 44829 (5B) worked the train to Carnforth, 70034 (9D) to Barrow where 45120 (12A) took over to Whitehaven. I moved on to Carlisle and, after a visit to Kingmoor (70003/6/53 stored), I decided to travel on to Dumfries to see two elusive black fives, 44699 and 44723, and luckily they were both on shed. I returned to Carlisle in time for the 1637 all stations to Skipton, headed by 44898 (12A) and, after enjoying the scenery (and a doze), I alighted at Long Preston where the lady porter kindly escorted me across the line to board the 1912 to Carnforth (44889-10J) from where I returned home behind 45095 (10A) on the 1708 from Workington.

Lead-up to 18 April 1966

Next afternoon, at Victoria there was the unusual sight of Britannias, on both the 1703 Blackpool (70017 – 9D) and the 1710 Southport (70014 – 5B) and I joined *Iron Duke* for the run to Wigan Wallgate, returning on the 1656 Liverpool Exchange to Bolton behind the now legendary 45318 (9K). I then went home for a few hours sleep as the next day (5 March) was the definite last, last day of the S&D. I journeyed south overnight, reaching Bath Green Park for the 0645 to Templecombe headed by 76026 (70F) and from there I then moved on to Salisbury to see 35028 on the S&D tour. On to Southampton where I joined the 0930 from Waterloo with 34097 to Bournemouth, then 75070 on the 1315 to Poole where I rejoined 76026 on the 1325 Branksome to Templecombe. This 2-6-0 had a very busy day as it later worked the 1550 to Evercreech Junction and the 1631 back down to Bournemouth! At Templecombe, the news was that the 1618 to Bath was to be worked by an 8F and 48760 duly appeared, so I joined the train for my last journey over this famous line. At Shepton Mallet, we had the colourful sight and exciting sound of unrebuilt Pacifics 34006/57 heading south into the afternoon sun, powering the LCGB Tour, followed by 80043 on the 1625 Bath to Templecombe. At Green Park, 80138 was waiting on the 1810 to Bournemouth but I had to head north after an enjoyable day, saddened by the loss of another wonderful line. I eventually reached Stockport and made a quick visit to Edgeley shed where there was an amazing array of motive power – 60019 (61B), 45596 and 70004/15/26!

Details were now filtering through of the changes from 18 April and DMUs were to take over the Leeds to Morecambe service, so on Monday 7 I spent the day travelling the route. I headed north behind 45312 (8B) on the 0600 Warrington to Carlisle up to Carnforth, then had 44667 (10J) on the 0810 to Skipton, 45445 (10J) on to Bingley (0929 Morecambe) and 45227 (10A) on the following 1035 from Carnforth into Leeds. After a meal break, I returned on

Lead-up to 18 April 1966

the 1352 from City (45227 after a quick turnaround) to Bingley, 44989 (12A) on the 1540 Bradford to Carlisle on to Skipton where I waited for the 1655 from Leeds headed by 45394 (10J). I travelled through to Morecambe returning with 45063 (55A) on the 1920 Leeds back to Carnforth and making for home behind 44795 (12A) on the 1708 from Workington.

On the seventeenth I travelled on some of my favourite mainline services that were soon to disappear. I set out on my usual diagram 0100 Exchange to Wigan with 73045 (9H), 45044 (6A ex-works) on the 0144 Crewe to Carnforth where *Britannia* itself took over on to Barrow. Here I planned to change to the 0600 Workmans to Sellafield (42134-12C) but, most unusually, another Pacific 70048 (12B) took over the 0144 so I stayed on to Foxfield before returning to Barrow for 44948 (10A) on the 0700 to Manchester. At Carnforth, I switched to the 0600 Warrington to Carlisle (45232 – 8B) to Oxenholme where I returned south behind 70014 (5B) working the 0810 Windermere to Manchester. Another Britannia (70022-12B) headed the 0815 Preston to Windermere before I finally returned south with 70000 (5B) on its return working, the 0900 Barrow to Euston.

The following week (twenty-fourth) the Pacifics were again out in force – 70031 (12B) on the 0810 Windermere, 70044 (9D) the 0900 Barrow, 70029 (12B) on the 1349 Crewe to Carlisle and even 70018 (5B) on the lightly loaded 1303 Workington to Manchester, but when D1850 failed at Preston on the 0900 Perth to Euston, Newton Heath five 44697 was given the Herculean task of starting the twelve-coach load unassisted. It valiantly crawled out of the station and disappeared in a cloud of smoke and steam – I wonder if it ever made Crewe.

Into April and after a late turn on Friday 1, I walked over to Exchange for the 0100 Glasgow headed by 45385 (8F) to

Lead-up to 18 April 1966

Wigan, then the 0144 Crewe (44761-5B) to Carnforth where 70000 (5B) again took over. It was now snowing heavily and when we arrived at Barrow it was thick on the ground, so I decided to play safe and return south. After watching 45372 (8F) depart on the 0530 to Whitehaven, I retired to the warmish waiting room, emerging when the stock of the 0700 to Manchester arrived, but the engine on the front was *Britannia* – still facing north! Apparently, the points on the turning triangle were frozen and, as no other loco was available, the Pacific had to work the train to Carnforth tender-first! Here it was uncoupled and headed for the turntable, but on the northbound relief line south of the station stood a long sleeping-car train, from which a Brush 4 was being removed by 46431 (10J), to be replaced by 45106 (12A) and an EE Type 4. As they headed north at 9 a.m. I could see the roofboards – Euston to Perth – which was actually due to be arriving there at 9 a.m.! The 0620 Carlisle to Crewe then rolled in behind 44897 (6B!) so we jumped on. At Lancaster we reboarded the 0700, now headed by 45393 (5B), down to Preston. Here, we found that the Blackpool locals were steam worked, 45444 (10D) had arrived from Blackpool South and we had 44822 (9D) out to Kirkham and returned on the first train back – headed by 48730 (10D)! I now had to make for work so I had 73096 (9H) on the 1110 from Windermere down to Warrington and my last sighting on this amazing day was of 45647 on the 0945 Newcastle to Liverpool!

On Thursday, 14 April, Liverpool were playing an evening match in Glasgow and the two supporters' specials were booked steam. I travelled to Liverpool exchange on the 0950 from Bolton behind 45408 (8F) and as we arrived both were preparing to leave, headed by 45395 (8F) and 45627 (8K). I considered trying to get on the Jubilee but there were just too many problems, so I watched them depart and then had 42611 (8F) back to Wigan Wallgate. I crossed to North Western and caught the 1110 Windermere to Crewe with

Lead-up to 18 April 1966

45097 (12A), returning north behind 70001 (12A) on the 1349 Crewe to Carlisle up to Carnforth, then 45061 (12A) back on the 1303 Workington to Manchester and, later, 70028 (5B) on the 1837 Crewe to Preston.

So, to the final weekend of the old timetable and, as it was impossible to cover everything, I just started travelling early on Friday 15 till late on Saturday 16. I began on the Liverpool–Rochdale line with 45385 (8F) on the 0735 Southport to Rochdale to Bury, where I waited for the following 0805 Southport, headed by 75043 (8L)), on to Rochdale. Sister engine 75048 (8K) was working the 0900 from Liverpool and I then viewed 70018 (5B) passing Bolton on the 0810 Windermere to Victoria. After lunch, I had 44728 (9K) on the 1315 Bolton to Liverpool, watched ex-works 70038 (12A) pound out of Wigan on the climb to the Boars Head with the 1349 Crewe to Carlisle, from Wallgate, before returning to Manchester for my last departure on the 1607 Barrow, powered by 44874 (10A) with nine on. How can a nine-coach train disappear from the timetable? This is rationalisation gone mad!

After 44874, 44873 (8F) was on the last 1625 Rochdale to Southport and the final 1722 Victoria to Windermere was unexpectedly worked by 45061 (12A), which had arrived on the previous day's 1303 from Workington, and not *Flying Dutchman* which brought in the 0810. I thought the Pacific may have been 'borrowed' for the Fridays-only York, but no, that had 44933 (9D). I now headed for Liverpool as this evening was also the last through-coach working from Euston to Southport. I left Manchester behind 45431 (8F) on the 1810 to Wigan, changing there into the 1858 Bolton to Liverpool with 44728 (9K) – having a busy day. We crossed 45104 (9K) on the 1740 Liverpool to Rochdale, followed by 42249 (9K) leading the 1805 Wigan. I eventually reached Edge Hill (no time for the chippy!) and watched clean 45156 (8M) back down on to the detached coaches and then

41

Lead-up to 18 April 1966

boarded for the journey to Southport – and another useful service had ended.

I then headed for Wigan where 45307 (8A) arrived on the 2235 from Lime Street, had 70027 (5B) on the 2345 Preston to Liverpool and then headed north behind 44683 (5B) on the 0144 from Crewe to Carnforth where 70024 (5B) took over to Barrow. I returned behind 45095 (10A) on the 0630 Preston and the last 0700 Barrow to Manchester was worked by 45328 (10A) – in fact, virtually every train was a last. At Lancaster, I joined 45015 (8A) on the 0600 Warrington to Carlisle back to Carnforth and then returned behind 70049 (12B) on the 0620 Carlisle to Crewe down to Preston where it was overtaken by the 0810 Windermere to Manchester. I just had time to take a last photograph of the two Britannias side by side before dashing to board the 0810 with 70040 (12A) on its last journey to Victoria. On the way we crossed the normally diesel 0900 Manchester to Glasgow but amazingly, on this of all days, it was headed by Newton Heath's 70021! I then returned to Preston for the 1235 to Windermere with 44915 (10J) to Lancaster, where I changed to 46514 (10J) on the 1318 to Carnforth, then 45446 (5B) on the 1425 Morecambe to Crewe back to Preston, returning north with 70011 (12B) on the 1349 Crewe to Carlisle. I then made a farewell journey on the little NW behind 45014 (10J – one of the shed's last working as it closed next day) on the 1620 Morecambe to Skipton where I waited for 45079 (55A) on the following 1700 from Carnforth through to Leeds. I dashed back to Manchester in time for the *Belfast Boat*, headed by 44837 (8A), to Bolton, where I joined 42587 (8F) on the 2035 to Wigan. I then made my weary way home, on the way catching a glimpse of 44817 (9J) on the last 2135 Rochdale to Liverpool and a large chunk of the North West's remaining steam passenger workings had ended.

Summer of 1966

18 April and the introduction of the full electric service from Euston to Crewe brought the inevitable transfer of diesels to the North West and DMUs took over the Rochdale to Liverpool and the Morecambe to Leeds services. The recasting of the West Coast timetable meant the disappearance of favourite trains like the 1607 Manchester Victoria to Barrow and the 1722 Victoria to Windermere. However, there *was* a silver lining – the Manchester Exchange to North Wales service reverted to loco-haulage and, though originally planned for Type 4s was almost completely steam worked till October.

On the eighteenth, I first checked the Central peak-hour departures and there was little change – 75060 (9F) on the 1712 and 1813 to Cheadle Heath, 45150 (9E) headed the 1722 to Buxton and 42697 (9E) the 1730 to Cheadle Heath plus the formerly DMU-operated 1740 to Chester Northgate was loco-hauled by 45116 (6A from 6B, as Mold Junction had just closed). On Wednesday 20, I checked the Exchange/Victoria workings – 73035 (9H) headed the 1510 to Bangor, 73160 (9H) the 1630 Llandudno Club and the 1605, 1710 and 1740 Southports remained steam as did the 1705 to Blackpool North with 70021 (9D) and the 1745 to Preston (Glasgow) worked by 45431 (8F).

On the West Coast, the 1346 Barrow to Crewe and the 1825 return were Britannia-hauled – 70039 (12A) headed the 1346 on the twenty-first – and Pacifics also appeared on the 1045 Exchange to Llandudno, 70025 (5B) on the twenty-seventh and 70023 (5B) on the twenty-eighth. The senior Llandudno Junction driver, who had worked in on the up Club with Patricroft standard fives, proffered the opinion that the 7MTs were 'too big for the service' while kindly giving me a footplate ride to Eccles.

Summer of 1966

Into May, and on the nineteenth Manchester United were playing an evening match at home. The first two specials from Central to Old Trafford were the usual fives – 45150 and 45404 – but the third was worked by 48535 (9E), most unusual by this time. The following evening I caught the 1737 (FO) Exchange to York with 44669 (12A) to Leeds, then had 45675 (55A) on the 2023 to Bradford (Forster Square) and crossed to Exchange for 61189 (56F) working the 2200 to Huddersfield.

The North Wales steam workings made visits to Chester more enjoyable and a typical day's travelling was on 7 June when I started with 73144 (9H) on the 1045 from Exchange, 45145 (6D) on the 1228 Chester to Wrexham, 44930 (8B) the 1312 back, 76036(6A) forward to Birkenhead, 45446 (5B) on the 1445 return, 45280 (6J) on the 1531 forward from Chester and 45353 (6A) back. I then had to suffer the 1755 DMU to Crewe, timetabled to arrive at 1826 but never (?) known to miss the connection into the 1825 Barrow which was powered by 70028 (5B). I alighted at Wigan (NW), crossed to Wallgate for 45385 (8F) on the 1900 Southport to Manchester Victoria and ended the day behind 45374 (10A) on the 2055 Heysham.

After work on Friday 17, I caught the 1737 (FO) from Exchange headed by 44903 (12A) and we had a good run from Huddersfield to Leeds in 26 minutes 58 seconds. I intended to travel on to York, but as we entered City station, 45593 (55A) was preparing to depart on the normally diesel-worked 1905 to Derby, so I hastily changed trains and savoured the Jubilee ride – a real surprise! Returning to Sheffield Midland for the 0200 to Leeds 44852(55A), I saw 45411 (9D) arrive on the 2255 (FO) Manchester Victoria to Yarmouth via the Hope Valley. I travelled on the 0200 to Normanton, then had 61030 (56A) on the 0210 from York to Halifax where 44846 (9D) took over on to Manchester. We alighted at Sowerby Bridge (not then aware of the Hebden

Bridge situation) changing to the 0420 from Manchester headed by 45425 (8F) to Normanton, where 61021 (50A) came on. We only travelled to the next station, Castleford, for on summer Saturdays there was an 0805 to Blackpool North – just time for a hot snack in the Beanery before returning to the station for 61013 (56A) on the Blackpool. I planned to travel through to Lancashire but while we were stopped at Wakefield 45739 (56A) arrived with an excursion to Bridlington – so, another hasty change of plan! The Jubilee worked throughout – via Hessle – and at Bridlington I caught a DMU on to Scarborough to catch the 1335 back to Manchester, expecting a Box, but it was headed by 61386 to Wakefield where 45425 took over on to Victoria.

Surprisingly, at the start of the summer timetable, the 1605 and 1740 Victoria to Southport reverted to DMUs but the short-dated extras like the 1850 from Southport were steam. The return working was the 2220 stopper on Monday to Thursday and the 1605 on Saturday after the stock had been used for the 0805 (SO) Exchange to Caernarvon and return! On Saturday 25, the returning Oldham wakes extras were double-headed from Victoria – 46412/45353 on the 0950 from Llandudno, 46501/45275 on a Rhyl relief and 44949/45280 on the Caernarvon. On the twenty-ninth, I travelled on the 1845 Southport to Oldham relief headed by 42079/44817 – terrific noise up to Werneth. On this evening there were three steam departures from Southport in 10 minutes as an 1840 Victoria extra had 45411 and the 1850 was worked by 42102 (8F).

For the summer service, Newton Heath lost all its Britannias – 70017/34 were transferred to Kingmoor, 70021/44 to Edgeley and 70000 had amazingly been withdrawn! On Friday 9 after work, I caught the 2255 from Victoria to Yarmouth via the Hope Valley. The train engine was 44938 (9D) with ten coaches, banked by 44891 (9D) up to Miles Platting. The five worked the train as far as Sheffield

Summer of 1966

Midland where there was a tight connection with what later became the Jubilee-worked 0225 Leeds to Glasgow but we missed it and had to wait for the 0200 to Leeds (44852-55A), then 42650 (56A) on the 0310 Normanton to Halifax, where 45076 (9D) took over to Manchester. Agecroft had two workings over Standedge and I caught the first – 44782 (9J) on the 0830 Scarborough to Stalybridge – where I waited for the second, 45096 (9J) on the 0900 Filey on to Huddersfield. Here, there was a wonderful choice: 45562 (55C) on the 0908 Leeds to Poole, followed by 45647 (55C) heading the 0915 Leeds to Llandudno. I joined *Sturdee* for the climb to Standedge and on to Stockport Edgeley where I switched to the return working (0914 Llandudno to Newcastle) headed by 44946 (56D) to Leeds and then returned to Manchester with 45005 (8A) on the 1355 Llandudno.

On the twelfth I tried to sample the performance of the 1346 Barrow to Crewe, starting out on the 1045 from Victoria to Blackpool North with 44697 (9D), I then returned to Preston and waited. 70040 (12A) arrived late on the Barrow and we crawled on to Wigan where the driver failed the Pacific and 45431 (8F) took over. Later, 70023 (5B) worked the 1825 from Crewe and 45455 (12A) headed the 1845 Windermere to Blackpool return excursion.

On Friday 23 I again travelled overnight on the 2255 Victoria to Yarmouth (with mobile tea trolley!) behind 45133 (9D) to Sheffield where 45675 (55A) was a welcome sight on the 0200 to Leeds. I travelled with Hardy to Normanton, then had 42204 to Wakefield (on the 0210 York where 43070 (56A) was working the 0515 to Barnsley and 0610 return – a rare working that I just had to sample. I then headed for York with 61199 (50A) on the 0420 from Manchester, then to Leeds where Jubilees were out in force: 45562 on the Poole, and 45647 the Llandudno before I joined 45593 on the 1015 to Glasgow. We departed 5 minutes late but steady climbing to Ribblehead (27.25 mph at Blea Moor Box) meant we reached

Summer of 1966

Appleby on time and we then made the tight connection at Carlisle into the Glasgow to Blackpool powered by 70032 (12B) over Shap to Preston, crossing 70011 (12B) heading the 1327 Manchester and Liverpool to Glasgow and 70012 (5B) the 1537 Crewe to Carlisle on the way.

While I was relaxing on Preston station, a succession of returning Accrington Wakes specials departed – 44679 (8F) and 44867 (9B) on a Poole relief, followed by 45421 (10D) and 45197 (10D) on another Poole and then 70026 (9B) on a Paignton extra. I then returned home with 44891 (9D) on the 1955 Blackpool North to Rochdale followed by 44868 (9B) on the 2050 Blackpool North to Manchester Victoria.

I had two weeks' holiday commencing on Saturday, 30 July and I booked a Scottish Rover for the first week, heading north the previous day on the 1327 (FO) from Victoria to Glasgow behind 44938 (9D). As we arrived at Preston, 45481 (12A) was ready to depart on a Barrow relief so I was able to catch this train to Lancaster and wait for the 1327 Liverpool to Glasgow there. I had heard that 45627 was active at Bank Hall but it was 45055 (8K) in charge – with eleven on! The five had just got going with its mammoth load when we suffered a signal stop at Carnforth – what kind of traffic regulation is this? From the restart 45055 reached 37.5 at Milnthrope before speed fell to 18.5 on the 1 in 111 at MP 18 and I was sure that the driver would take a pilot from Oxenholme but no, he bravely carried on unassisted and reached 25.75 on the 1 in 106 to Grayrigg. Unfortunately, due to an unexpected interruption I had to cease logging, but we then crawled up to Shap Summit unaided and eventually reached Carlisle, crossing 70002 (12A) on the 1400 from Glasgow. The exhausted black five was replaced by 70038 (12A) which took a banker (42058) up to Beattock summit and at Carstairs I joined the Edinburgh portion worked by 45469 (64C). I returned to Carstairs at 2110 behind 44954 (66B) and then headed north on the 2025 Carlisle to Perth

Summer of 1966

with 70003. I alighted at Stirling to wait for the 2300 Glasgow to Aberdeen expecting an A4 but 60532 (61B) was in charge.

I travelled through to Aberdeen and then trekked to Ferryhill to discover that the only A4 in steam was 60024, 60019 was under repair and 60004/9 were in store! I returned to the station for a sleep in the 0620 stock and awoke to the sound of an engine backing on to the stock – it was *Kingfisher*! We reached a max of 72 between Coupar Angus and Perth, where I got off to be informed of an 0910 Dundee to Edinburgh relief rostered to be worked by 60919 (62B). The V2 had six coaches on and made a lot of noise but speed fell to thirty-two at Lochmuir and only twenty at Dysart! From Waverley, I had 73108 (66E) to Carstairs, and 70001 into Glasgow on the 0820 from Morecambe before heading south on the return working to Carlisle, double-headed by 73105 (67A) and 45025 (10A). Here, 70002 was working throughout on the 1327 from Liverpool but I waited for the 0920 from St Pancras and was rewarded with 45675 (55A) on an eight-coach load. We roared our way to Dumfries with 62 at Racks, stopped at New Cumnock for water, and at Kilmarnock we acquired 77019 (67B) as a pilot for the climb to Lugton. From Glasgow, I headed for Edinburgh (noting 60034 on Eastfield shed) and then had 73108 (66B) and 44669 (12A) on the 2340 to the south. I fell asleep and woke at Carlisle where there was a succession of northbound reliefs. The first two arrived behind 70012 and 70011, to be replaced by 70041 and 70003 but they were wedged so I decided to wait. Three more specials arrived, all double-headed by class fives (including Patricroft's 73144, 45064 (6E) and 45280 (6J)) but they were all replaced by diesels so I had to catch the last one – at least I had a sound sleep!

The only Sunday steam passenger working that I knew of was the 2005 Dundee to Glasgow, so I spent the day on a mini shed bash, including Dunfermline and St Margarets, before relaxing in the warm sunshine at Waverley Gardens and promptly

Summer of 1966

falling asleep. I woke too late to reach Dundee, so I had to make for Gleneagles and catch the 2005 there, headed by 44720 (63A). On arrival at Buchanan Street and still feeling weary, I enquired about bed and breakfast and was directed to a nearby establishment where I was asked to pay in advance – maybe they'd had English 'neverers' here before!

On Monday morning, the 0825 was a box so I tried the Gourock line but no steam there either, and I could only get to Larbert for the 1330 from Aberdeen – headed by the immaculate *Blue Peter*. I then had 73149 (65B) on the 1735 from Buchanan Street to Callender, returning with 73153 (65B) on the 1530 from Aberdeen on which I was informed that the Ayr to Kilmarnock locals were being steam-worked this week, so I dashed down to Ayr and had 77007 (67B) on the 2105 to Drybridge and 76074 (67C) back. I then went to Girvan for the up *Northern Irishman* worked by 70016 (piloted by 44788 to Ayr) through to Carlisle and returned on the down *Northern Irishman* with 70040, piloted from Ayr to Stranraer by 44788. Returning to Ayr, I spent a sunny morning photographing and travelling behind 77018/9 on the Kilmarnock locals before heading for Perth and *Blue Peter* on the 1330 Aberdeen back to Glasgow.

Next morning (3 August), I had 44997 (63A) on the 0715 from Perth as far as Alyth Junction and waited for the 0620 from Aberdeen, but no A4 – it was headed by 44703 (61B). However, there was news of another V2 working that evening on an 1840 Edinburgh to Dundee relief, so after fitting in the Corstorphine branch on the 1718 from Waverley behind 45168 (64A), I joined 60813 (64a) on the relief with six on and lots of off-beat roar to Dundee.

Later, I had 70040 on the 2025 Carlisle to Perth and 60532 on the 2300 through to Aberdeen where I slept in the 0620 stock and returned to Perth with 44703 and 44997 double-headed.

Summer of 1966

Next day (my last), there was a 1945 Aberdeen to Edinburgh relief worked by the ever-reliable 44703, after which I bade farewell to Scotland with 45483 (64A) on the 2340 to Carstairs. At Carlisle, 70005 was on the down Stranraer and 70016 on the up and 45697 arrived on the 0225 from Leeds. I headed south behind 70022 (12B) on the 0750 to Crewe, then later 70047 on the 1047 Preston to Barrow, returning behind 45376 (8A) on the 1433 from Barrow and then 70018 on the 1400 from Glasgow to Preston from where I returned home with 44818 (9D) on the Manchester portion.

The next day (Sunday) I visited Agecroft, where a batch of former Nuneaton 8Fs had arrived – even though the shed was being run down for closure in October! Locos stored included 44781!, 47201 and Patricroft's 73000/25/34/50/67.

For the second week of my holiday I booked a Southern Rover and travelled down overnight to Euston and then crossed to Waterloo for the 0718 to Salisbury, headed by 73119. I returned to London behind 34089 on the 0649 from Salisbury and then had 35008 on the 1030 down followed by 34037 on the 1130 from Waterloo and 34066 working the 1424 Weymouth to Eastleigh. Later I had 34077 on the 2213 Weymouth to Waterloo as far as Bournemouth where 34018 took over. I returned behind 34071 on the 0245 down and then 34100 on the 0530 from Waterloo. At Basingstoke, I studied the morning action; successive up trains were hauled by 73085/86/88 and 73087 was on the 0718 Waterloo to Salisbury. I then headed west behind 73029 on the 0930 down, then 34087 on the 1130 and 34002 worked the 1330 down. I then watched 34025 leave Bournemouth on the up *Belle* before heading for the nearby café for a much-needed hot meal. I noticed a card in the window advertising bed and breakfast so, needing a good night's sleep, I enquired inside and it was the Italian waitress herself who was offering the accommodation, so I booked the next three nights. In the evening, I caught the 2124 to Brockenhurst (34098) to return

Summer of 1966

on the 1930 from Waterloo behind 35030 before retiring, exhausted!

Next morning (tenth) I headed for Swanage, starting with 75065 on the 0930 Bournemouth to Weymouth to Poole, picking up 34098 on the 0921 from Weymouth back and then down with 73043 on the 1049 from Bournemouth to Wareham. I had 41316 (70F) down to Swanage and later returned with 80032, then on to Weymouth behind 76064, crossing 35030 on the 1325 up. I returned from Weymouth on the 1550 with 73065 to Brockenhurst and headed down to Lymington behind 41230 (70F). I then had 34098 on the 1730 down, followed by 34017 on the 1830 from Waterloo and finally 35013 on the 2015 from Weymouth before heading for my digs. The following morning I started on the 0921 from Weymouth headed by 34034 and returned from Southampton on the 1030 Waterloo behind 34036. I headed back to Southampton with 34006 on the 1259 from Bournemouth, noted 35013 on the down *Belle*, before catching 76031 into Portsmouth. I then headed for Southampton Terminus and had 76059 on the 1817 to Central, returning to Bournemouth with 34034 on the 1730 from Waterloo.

Friday dawned, and I began the long journey home – could I get steam all the way? I began with 35027 on the 0730 Weymouth to Waterloo and with eleven on speed fell to 45 at New Milton and then a max of 72 after Brockenhurst so I alighted at Southampton and waited for the following 0846 from Bournemouth, headed by 34037, but the highlight of this run was the sight of an immaculate 60532 on Basingstoke shed! 34060 was on the 1230 down, but I crossed London to Marylebone for the 1438 worked by 44858 with only four coaches. I rode to Loughborough, returned to Leicester with 44811 and there caught 44876 on the 1720 from Rugby. The load was only three coaches but I started logging and we rocketed away, passing Rothly at 69, Quorn at 78.5 and, timed on rail-joints, I recorded a 90 maximum before severe braking into Loughborough, reached in 10 minutes 16 seconds – just over even time! Here, I had a quick word with the driver who told me that he did it 'for a friend' – must be a new chat-up line! I returned to Leicester with 45222 and then 44847 on the 1638 from Marylebone which with a load of four and a van reached Loughborough in 11 minutes 23 seconds the GC was going out in style! I then had a long wait at Nottingham Victoria for the 2343 to Sheffield Victoria hauled by 45289, crossed to Midland for 45219 on the 0200 to Leeds, as far as Normanton, 61013 on the 0210 York to Manchester to Wakefield, 42204 down to Barnsley and back and then 45395 on the 0420 from Manchester to Normanton where 61337 took over on to York. Unfortunately, I had to suffer diesel to Leeds but was rewarded on arrival by the sight of 45647 on the Poole and 45562 on the Llandudno which I travelled on to Huddersfield where I waited for Agecroft's best black five, 45096, on the 0830 from Scarborough. With eight on, we stormed up to Standedge, entering the tunnel at 47.5, and with a max of 68 at Mossley we reached Stalybridge in just over 28 minutes, then on to Victoria in 12 minutes 50 seconds. I then just had time to have 44856 out to Rochdale on the Llandudno to Bradford (banked by 46437) before dashing back to work for a late turn!

The following week the 0758 Accrington to Victoria and the return 1722 to Blackburn reverted to steam from DMU, and on Friday 19 I travelled behind 45196 (10F) on the 1722 via Entwistle, which by then was rare with steam. I moved on to Preston where 70028 arrived on the 1400 Glasgow to Liverpool and I returned home on the Manchester portion with 44818 (9D). Next morning, Saturday, I caught the 0900 to Filey from Exchange with 44782 (9J) and this turned out to be the last time that was hauled by an Agecroft loco, though the performance did not match the occasion as we took over 17 minutes to Stalybridge (with ten on) and at Huddersfield the driver failed the five which was replaced by

Summer of 1966

45445 (10A). I alighted here and changed platform for the arrival of Farnley's Jubilees – *Alberta* on the Poole, then *Sturdee* on the Llandudno. My problem now was that I was starting work at 3 p.m. so I had to chose 45647 which, with eleven on, suffered a signal stop before Longwood but then roared up to Standedge reaching 29 at Marsden. I intended to get off at Stalybridge as the Llandudno was not booked to stop at Chester, but I decided to stay on and chance my luck. We were banked by 92126 (8B) from Arpley to Acton Grange and then, entering Chester Station, we were routed into the platform and stopped! Apparently an elderly lady had got on the wrong train and the special stop was arranged for her, but I just had to take advantage of this opportunity to get to work on time, and though challenged by a golden, I just kept on walking and returned on the 1140 from Llandudno with 73073 (9H) to Warrington and then 44866 on the 1145 Caernarvon to Manchester.

The following weekend was the August Bank Holiday, so after work on Friday night I caught the overnight mails to Leeds where 45697 (55A) was working the 0225 to Carlisle. With seven on, we departed 40 minutes late and had two signal steps at Whitehall Junction – was this deliberate? After Skipton, we reached 55 through Hellifield but I must have dozed off, for my log ends there! At Carlisle, I had 70038 (12B) on the 0750 to Crewe, changed to 70049 (12B) on the 0830 from Barrow (banked from Lancaster by 46400 off the 0920 from Morecambe) and headed home behind 73157 (9H) on the 0938 Morecambe to Manchester Victoria. On the Monday, I worked on early and then went to Exchange where 45647 (55C) had arrived on the 1315 from Llandudno (plus lots of enthusiasts) and I joined them on the 1630 to Llandudno with 73141 (9H) to Colwyn Bay and returned on Llandudno to Rock ferry special headed by 42942 (8H) with ten coaches! I then returned to Manchester with 44917 (6A) on the 2055 from Chester and on arrival I was surprised to see 45368 (8F) waiting to leave on the 2220 stopper to

Summer of 1966

Southport with eight on (the 1710 club stock which must have been used for an earlier relief) so I jumped aboard for the short ride to Pendleton.

All too soon the last weekend of the summer timetable arrived and on the Friday (2 September) I headed for Preston behind 44846 (9D) on the 1045 to Blackpool North, and with seven on we stormed over Hilton House at 37.5 mph. At Preston, 70029 (12B) was working the 0825 Glasgow to Liverpool (diesel failure?) and 44809 was on the Manchester portion. 44911 (12A) arrived on the 1100 from Windermere – but what was working the 1327 Liverpool to Glasgow? Well, it wasn't 45627 which rolled in on the Blackpool, but I turned down the Jubilee and waited. The 1327 arrived with 45055 again which with the Manchester portion added had eleven on – Bank Hall must really rate this black five! The run to Lancaster was ruined by PWSs at Garstang and Bay Horse, but from there the engine and crew really tried with this heavy load – 62 through Carnforth, falling only to 56.5 at Burton box, 45 past Hincaster Junction and, disdaining assistance, pounding through Oxenholme at 37.5. Speed fell to 25.5 at Mosedale Hall, 28.5 at Grayrigg and accelerating after Low Gill, we were obviously going to tackle Shap unassisted! Pounding through Tebay at 55.5, we dropped to 26 at Scout Green and topped the summit at 18.5 mph. On arrival at Penrith, it was a pleasure to thank this game crew and their sturdy class five before returning south on the 1400 from Glasgow headed by 70054 (12A). With eleven on, the Pacific topped Shap at 37.5 but a PWS at Lambrigg and a signal stop at Burton restricted the running afterwards. I alighted at Preston and waited for the return of the Blackpool to Liverpool and *Sierra Leone* and with seven on (and after a signal stop at Moss Lane Junction), the Jubilee sustained 75 through Rufford and 74 at Maghull before signals at Old Roan, and I am still wondering how 45627 would have fared on the 1327.

Summer of 1966

So, to the last Saturday and I headed for a rare working – the 0945 Piccadilly to Yarmouth hauled by 45073 (9E) with ten on via the Hope Valley. We reached 53 at Marple Wharf Junction, had a severe signal check at Chinley North Junction and then an enjoyable journey through the scenic countryside with a max of 69.25 at Hope. At Sheffield Midland, the Yarmouth made a convenient connection with the Leeds to Poole and, yes, it was *Alberta*. The driver got the 'Right-away!' but we didn't move – the Jubilee had apparently stopped dead level (with three cylinders?) and the loco wouldn't roll back either. It seemed an age before we finally got moving and soon the familiar Jubilee roar began as we pounded up to Broadway tunnel reaching 58 through Dronfield and 69 at Sheepbridge before settling down to a more sedate pace on to Nottingham, where I jumped off to watch the Jubilee uncouple. Would we ever see one working again?

With the end of the summer timetable came more bad news – the North Wales services (except for the Club) were to revert to DMU and Llandudno Junction shed was to close from 2 October. On 15 September I finished an early turn at 3 p.m. and dashed to Exchange just in time to dive into the last coach of the 1510 Bangor, and not till Warrington was I able to check the engine. As I approached the end of the platform, I was warmly greeted by a very famous Patricroft fireman who invited me on to the footplate of Caprotti 73127 (9H) for the journey on to Chester! As we arrived here, the crew asked how I was returning and when I replied that I would have to wait for the 1637 Holyhead (maybe box) they invited me to join them on their next working – the Stanlow to Stourton oil tanks – so I followed them along the track to the loco, 9F 92069 (8H). I wasn't able to assess the weight of the load but the climb on the 1 in 100 to Guilden Sutton was hard work for both engine and crew but from there we sailed along and the 2-10-0 rode very smoothly. All too soon we reached Patricroft station and the driver slowed down so

Summer of 1966

that I could jump off – what a marvellous experience with a wonderful crew.

On Friday 23, I heard that a Birkenhead 'Crab' would be on evening passenger work, so I headed for Chester on the 1045 from Exchange, unusually worked by 44759 (5B). I returned to Warrington with 73073 (9H) on the 1140 from Llandudno then back with 44873 (8F) on the 1510 Manchester to Bangor, which suffered four signal checks on to Chester! I then had 76062 (6A) to Birkenhead and 42087 (8H) back before retiring to the refreshment room. I emerged for the 2108 to Birkenhead powered by a very clean 42782 (8H) and I enjoyed this now rare motive power to Rock ferry. I crossed the river for the 2235 Lime Street to Wigan headed by 45242 (8A) and then boarded the northbound *Northern Irishman* and fell asleep – waking on the approach to Carlisle. 70010 (12A) took over the *Northern Irishman* but I headed back south behind 70013 (12B) on an extra/relief and before we departed 70008/34 and 45274 were also heading up reliefs – was it *Blackpool Illuminations*? I travelled down to Preston with *Oliver Cromwell* and there waited for the 0610 from Blackpool to Euston, hauled by 44767 (12A) with ten coaches and thirty-ton van. The unique five reached 47.5 at Leyland and 56 at Balshaw Lane before a signal check on the descent into Wigan, but from here we had a clear run to Warrington reached in 14 minutes 58 seconds with 45 max after Golbourne. I was tempted to stay on to Crewe but decided to concentrate on North Wales and had 45247 (6J) on the 0740 from Manchester on to Chester and then a very sprightly run behind 73053 (9H) on to Prestatyn on the following 0830 Manchester. With eight on (244 tons), the standard five reached 64.75 at Saltney Ferry and touched 72 at Mostyn taking 26 minutes 53.5 seconds – just failing to make even time. I returned to Chester with 45345 (6E) on an up relief and on to Manchester (and work) with 45044 (6A) on the 1140 from Llandudno.

Summer of 1966

So, into the last week of North Wales steam and on Monday 26 I again headed to Exchange for the 1510 Bangor to be greeted by another friendly Patricroft crew who invited me straight on to the footplate. The driver was very keen and with only five coaches we reached Newton in 18 minutes 18 seconds (71 max at Parkside), then hopelessly checked on to Warrington but from there to Chester, with only one check and via the old line to Walton, we took 22 minutes 22 seconds. The loco was 45001 (6J). The Stourton Tanks was not running and the crew returned passenger, so I caught 73140 (9H) on the 1720 Wrexham and 45466 (8C) back.

On Thursday I again had a footplate ride from exchange on the 1510 aboard 45231 (6A), a free-running engine and, with the same five on, we reached 70 at Astley followed by a prolonged 75 to Kenyon Junction before a slight signal check at Parkside, and we stopped in Newton-le-Willows in 17 minutes 12 seconds – a record for me. We had a clear run on to Warrington reached in 9 minutes 10 seconds (another personal best) and from there to a signal stop outside Chester station in 20.5 minutes. On arrival, I heartily thanked the crew for two wonderful rides and a terrific performance.

Next day (Friday), I started on the 1737 (FO) from Exchange to York headed by 70029 (12B) with eight on but we took over 15 minutes to Stalybridge (a minute slower than my best black five run) and then, after 45 at Saddleworth, we suffered a signal stop at Diggle! On the way, we crossed 45562 (55C) on the 1728 Leeds to Blackpool North weekend excursion, which was booked non-stop from Huddersfield on the outward journey but on the Sunday return it very handily stopped at Victoria for water. I left the Britannia at Leeds, where 75042 (10G) was unusual on the 2001 to Skipton, and later I had 61131 (56A) on the 2125 Bradford Exchange to Wakefield. Another B1 61237 (56A) headed the

Summer of 1966

2200 to Huddersfield and later I was again pulled by it on the next leg of the diagram, the 0310 Normanton to Halifax, where 44891 (9D) took over as the 0438 to Manchester. Our normal practice was to alight at Sowerby Bridge and wait for the 0420 from Manchester but in theory we could travel on to Hebden Bridge and change there. But what would be the reception at this out-of-the-way station? We decided to find out, and on arrival we grouped together and approached the solitary porter who enquired, 'Where have you lads come from?' 'Wakefield,' we replied, and he then asked, 'Where are you going to?' 'Back to Wakefield,' we answered. 'Well you'll want t'other platform then,' was his logical response – and so the great Hebden Bridge 'saga' began, but that's another story!

The 0420 rolled in behind 44679 (8F) as far as Normanton but from here I headed back to Manchester to savour the last day of the service to North Wales. At Exchange, 73011 (H) arrived on the 0740 from Llandudno and I travelled to Chester on the last 1045 down with 73073 (9H), then 44831 (6J) to Wrexham and 44917 (6A) back, on to Warrington for the last 1510 Manchester to Bangor headed by 44981 through to Flint and, finally, 73159 (9H) on the 1735 Manchester to Llandudno. I then wearily headed for home, having enjoyed a wonderful last week, but I now had to bid farewell to the last summer of steam from Manchester to North Wales.

From Winter into Spring 1967

The end of 1966 meant further heavy blows for Manchester's steam enthusiasts. Friday, 30 December was the last Llandudno Club – 0740 up and 1630 Exchange return – and by special request, double-chimneyed black five 44766 (6A) was provided. I went out to Warrington for the up working and, with a ten-coach load, we reached 72 at Astley but a signal-stop at Cross Lane meant we arrived 5 minutes late – the nett time was just over 29 minutes. I then headed for Preston and returned to Victoria behind 44910 (8L) on the 1212 (0825 Glasgow) – Aintree had taken over the working after the closure of Bank Hall.

At Central, the remaining steam workings over the Hope Valley were being dieselised from 1 January and the Cheadle Heath's were being withdrawn, so I caught the 1530 to Sheffield with 44807 (6A!) and saw 45448 (9F) preparing to work the 1712 and 1813 to Cheadle Heath for the last time. I then returned to Victoria for, even though the 1705 (SX) Blackpool North and 1710 (SX) Southport Clubs were to remain steam-hauled for another week, I chose to make my farewell trip to Southport on this Friday and cover the Blackpool on the last day. 45048 (8F) worked the 1710 with the usual seven-coach rake of Mark Is but a signal check at Deal Street meant a slow climb to Pendlebury and the max before Atherton was only 60 before the PWS. We had a clear road after Wigan and speed was in the high 60s from Parbold to after Bescar Lane – but no flying farewell to this racing ground. I returned to Victoria and had 45444 (10D) on the *Belfast Boat* with ten and a van on but slipping at the start, more signals at Deal Street and a severe PWS at Kearsley ruined the climb.

59

From Winter into Spring 1967

Rising very early next morning (thirty-first), I caught the 0425 to York hauled by 45441 (8C) to Normanton, then down to Sheffield Midland for a last ride over the Hope Valley on the 0915 to Chinley. This was Buxton shed's last passenger working and they had turned out 46492 (9L) in very clean condition. I sat back and enjoyed the scenery before continuing on to Central for yet another last – the 1255 (SO) to Cheadle Heath worked by 44830 (9F) with a rake of Southern green stock! I then returned to Manchester and work, but during an evening meal break I nipped into Central to see 42071 (9E) bring in the ECS of the 2000 to Sheffield and watched 44851 (9E) depart into the night with it, so ending Hope Valley passenger steam – and 1966.

Into 1967 and Central now had only one scheduled steam departure, the 1725 to Buxton, and on Monday, 2 January I sampled 45269 (9E) on this train. As we departed, I noticed that the 1740 to Chester Northgate was loco-hauled – by a standard five, presumably one of Patricroft's. This train had been DMU for many years but was quite often steam and the next morning 44917 (6A) brought in the up working – the 0721 from Chester. I then concentrated on the Victoria Clubs: on Tuesday, 3 January, 44697 (9D) worked the 1705 and 44963 (8B) the 1710 and on Thursday I rode out to Wigan on the 1710 with 45134 (10A). So Friday arrived – the last scheduled day of steam haulage for both trains. I arrived at Victoria before 1700 and, standing on Platform Eleven, I watched as they rolled in simultaneously from Red Bank headed by two Newton Heath stalwarts – 44891 into Platform Twelve on the Blackpool and 44845 into eleven on the Southport. I had already decided to travel on the 1705 but the running was moderate – not helped by a signal stop after Walkden before tackling the climb to Hilton House. (Fortunately, I *did* have a wonderful run on this train on its *next*, very last time steam on 12 April behind 45203 (9D) and a game crew!)

From Winter into Spring 1967

The following Friday (the thirteenth!), I headed for Leeds on the 1734 (FO) from Exchange behind 70047 (12A) – but no Jubilees working from Holbeck. 44828 (55A) was on the 2001 to Skipton, so I went to Bradford (Forster Square) with 42699 (55A) on the 2025, returning on the 2130 behind 42093 (55F).

The next day, Saturday 14, I spent the afternoon on the Chester to Shrewsbury line and 45116 (6A) was on the 1531 but not the 'total thrash' run. I returned with 45323 (8B) and then caught the famous 1755 DMU to Crewe due to arrive at 1826 – officially a minus one-minute connection with the 1825 Barrow but never (?) missed! 70006 (12A) had nine and a van on the 1825, reaching 75 at Acton Bridge before signals. I had intended to alight at Preston (where the load was reduced to three and a van) but must have dozed off there waking as we tore through Garstang at 78, accelerating rapidly, reaching 92 (twice) after Oubeck! Obviously this performance took Lancaster by surprise as we suffered a signal-stop at number four box! The actual was 21 minutes 35 seconds but the nett was probably little over 18 minutes.

There was a surprise on the sixteenth, when a Britannia, 70048 (12A) worked the down *Belfast Boat* but any chance of a record climb to Kearsley was ruined by the 20 mph PWS there. The 1722 Buxton was now regularly worked by 44665 (9E), but on Friday (twentieth) I switched to the 1734 (FO) York and was rewarded with 45028 (12A) to Leeds and then 45647 on the 2001 to Skipton, returning with 42072 (55F) on the 2130 from Forster Square. The overnight York Mails was now diesel and as a result 70026/44 were in store at Stockport Edgeley.

The 1825 Crewe was still Britannia worked, 70049 (twenty-fourth) and 70041 (twenty-fifth) but the next day (twenty-sixth) I was working a 2 p.m. late turn, so I had just enough time to pick up the 0825 Glasgow from Bolton. Announced

From Winter into Spring 1967

as 20 minutes late, I had almost decided to return by DMU when 45107 (10D) rolled in only 15 minutes down – with the Preston driver who had once taken the 0810 Windermere through Clifton Junction at 70! With 70N (233.5 tons), we cleared Moses Gate in 3 minutes 3 seconds and then tore down Kearsley to touch 72 at MP5 and, with very little braking, another 70 through Clifton (50 restriction!) but smooth riding, yet I had been round at 72 with Bolton's Mad Hatter when I felt that we were coming off the rails, so the Preston man knew the exact safe limit. We then passed Agecroft Junction at 72 and still at 69 through Pendleton before the inevitable signals and a signal stop at Windsor Bridge number one – reached in 10 minutes 34 seconds from Bolton. Allowing 4.25 minutes from Windsor Bridge number three to Victoria, the nett time was approximately 13.5 minutes! Needless to say, I arrived on time for work.

On Friday 27, 70010 (12A) worked the 1734 (FO) to Leeds, from where I went to Bradford for 44990 (56F) on the 2125 to Wakefield. Returning to Manchester, I went overnight with 73160 (9H) on the 0100 Exchange to Wigan, caught the Barrow sleeper which, at Carnforth, was taken over by 44905 (10A) and 44832 (5B). They returned on the 0715 from Barrow and I travelled back to Carnforth from where I headed north to Carlisle as the local football team were playing a cup match at Blackburn and there were three excursions – all booked for Britannias.

70012 worked the 1031 with 130N via Shap, 70014 the 1040 (eleven on) via Ais Gill and I travelled throughout on the last – 70003 at 1050 with 110N via Shap. From a Penrith stop, we reached 39 at the summit and then 82 through Tebay before a signal stop at Hincaster Junction. That day, Central Lancashire was overrun with football specials as Liverpool were playing at Burnley with six excursions (all black fives) and Aston Villa at Preston. I rode down to Crewe on this return working behind 45273 (55A).

From Winter into Spring 1967

By now the Manchester sheds had very large allocations for – as other areas dieselised or depots closed – any serviceable locos were transferred en masse. For example, Patricroft received 8Fs from Colwick and standard fives from Nuneaton and many engines were in store – including the still ex-works 73134 which after overhaul at Cowlairs in July 1965 (and then famously working from Ayr shed) had been mothballed – fuelling rumours of a strategic reserve. Over at Central, 44665 had disappeared (apparently for a light-overhaul) and on Monday 30 I had a good run on the 1725 with 44804 (9E) which made Chinley in 25 minutes 29 seconds, on to Chapel in 4 minutes 20 seconds and Peak Forest in 6 minutes 11 seconds. However, on the following evening, I missed the reappearance of 44665, which got to Chinley in 23.5 minutes!

I had the following weekend off work so on Friday, 3 February, I headed for the Cambrian – to Shrewsbury with 44917 on the 1228 Chester, then 75033 on the down Cambrian cost to Aberystwyth and back with the 1815 mails. I returned to Chester with 45353 (6A) on the 2148 Shrewsbury and moved on to Crewe. The Welsh rugby team were playing in Edinburgh the next day and, maybe, the excursions would be steam, so I walked out to Gresty Lane but the type fours worked right through!

I returned to the station where the good news was that 70013 had left the works and was running in on the Preston duty! I headed north on the Barrow sleepers and waited for the Pacifics return working – the 0535 passenger to Crewe. At last *Oliver Cromwell* rolled in, looking immaculate – fully lined-out and painted jet black underneath. I climbed aboard and relaxed, dozing off a few times as we made leisurely progress on an easy schedule before, all too soon, the journey was over.

I then headed for Birkenhead to catch the 0855 Paddington – 42647 to Chester and 45145 (6D) from there – then 45285 (6D) on the 1228 Chester, back with 44831 (6A)

From Winter into Spring 1967

on the 1225 Shrewsbury, 45310 (6D) 1345 to Birkenhead and 42647 (again) on the 1445 return. At Chester, 45116 (6A) took over the six-coach (204 ton) train and, as I had never had a fast run with this loco, I wasn't expecting fireworks. The front coach was well stocked with enthusiasts, including many from the South who had forsaken their Bullied Pacifics to sample Northern performance! We left 4 minutes late and had a good run to Wrexham in 18 minutes 9 seconds, even better to Ruabon in 6 minutes 51 seconds with 60 at Bersham box, and on to Gobowen in 9 minutes 32 seconds with 65 max at Cefn, arriving 2.5 minutes late. The driver had already been well chatted but was now offered even more inducement to beat the mile-a-minute schedule to Shrewsbury – in 17 minutes if possible! 45116 rocketed away from Gobowen, the exhaust sounding like a machine-gun, and we passed Whittington in under 3 minutes and Haughton box in 6 minutes 18 seconds (even time) touching 87 mph – but the engine couldn't take this thrashing and with injector problems, Driver Webb had no alternative but to ease down for the remainder of the journey. Even so, he only just failed to break 17 minutes and the heroic crew received a well-deserved, generous whip-round before we raced over to the down side where 45089 (6A) was waiting impatiently to depart on the 1637 back to Chester. Here, we all piled into the 1755 to Crewe – a two-car DMU wedged full of enthusiasts! There was no danger of missing the connection this evening as the 1825 Barrow was running 25 minutes late – headed by 70016 (12A) with eleven on, approximately 400 tons. The crew made a valiant effort to recover lost time, reaching 80 at Hartford and not falling below this speed to near Acton Grange, with a maximum of 85 after Acton Bridge and a time of 26 minutes 14 seconds to Warrington. The run on to Wigan was bedevilled by signal checks which must have disheartened the driver for we made a weak climb to the Boars Head and only 66.5 max down to Preston. By now I had been travelling for thirty-six hours, so, weary, I forsook the dash to Lancaster and headed home –

secure in the knowledge that I had experienced a truly memorable day in the 'decline of steam'.

45116 (6A) six on 204 tons
1531 Chester to Paddington (4 February 1967)

Miles				
–	Gobowen	depart	0000	(3 mins late)
1–8	Whittington	pass	0253	68
4–8	Rednal	pass	0512	80/85
6–5	Haughton box	pass	0618	87
10–5	Baschurch	pass	0935	75 (eased)
14–3	Leaton	pass	1237	72
	Coton Hills	pass	1551	
18	Shrewsbury	arrive	1706	(schedule 18 mins)

70016 (12A) 11 on 400 tons (approx)
1825 Crewe to Barrow (4 February 1967)

Miles				
–	Crewe	depart	0000	(25 mins late)
–	Copp Junction	pass	0701	
7–5	Winsford	pass	1119	
12–0	Hartford	pass	1448	80
14–5	Acton Bridge	pass	1658	85
–	Weaver Junction	pass	1828	81
–	Norton Crossing		2048	82
	Acton Grange		2243	
24–0	Warrington	arrive	2614	

On Saturday, 11 February, I headed for Yorkshire on the 0425 from Victoria (73158 – 9H) to Normanton (crossing 45083 (9D) on the 0210 York to Manchester Victoria) and 43140 (55B) took over to York. On to Leeds for 42189 (55F) on the

From Winter into Spring 1967

1015 to Bradford (Forster Square), a dash to Exchange for 42235 (56F) on the 1100 to Leeds Central, and finally to Harrogate for 44896 (55A) on the 1250 back to Leeds, before returning to Manchester and work.

On Monday (thirteenth), I spent the afternoon between Chester and Wrexham before making for Crewe and the 1825, headed by a grimy black five – 44933 (8A) – with ten on. We took over 30 minutes to reach Warrington, struggled on to Wigan before the five made a powerful effort on the climb to the Boars Head, reaching 33.5 mph at the top of the 1 in 104, bettering most Pacific performances, but signal checks between Balshaw Lane and Leyland was a poor reward for this sterling climb. On to Lancaster, the Carnforth crew tried hard (68 at Oubeck) but 44933 just couldn't run though it could certainly pull!

My next Chester trip was on 23 February, when I had planned an early start to catch the 0933 – but I overslept after a very late turn the day before and my first ride was behind 44831 (6A) on the 1228 through to Shrewsbury. Here I was told the amazing news that on the 0933, 44917 had reached a record breaking 96 at Haughton! To recover, I flopped into the down *Cambrian* and had 75033 to Aberystwyth and back.

On Saturday (twenty-fifth), 70010 (12A) worked the 1825 Crewe with ten on reaching Warrington in 26 minutes 59 seconds (76 Max after Weaver Junction) and the next evening I sampled the 2338 Liverpool (Line St) to Leeds behind 73128 (9H) reaching Victoria in 45 minutes 59 seconds and a max of 72 after Glazebury. 45431 (8F) was working the 0100 Exchange to Glasgow but I headed home. On Monday evening (twenty-seventh), I again went to Crewe for the 1825 but 70024 (12A) took over 28 minutes to reach Warrington, so I detrained and headed for Manchester and the *Belfast Boat*. Maybe I should have stayed on, for this

From Winter into Spring 1967

proved to be my last steam run on the Barrow – another star working gone.

Into March 1967, and the last steam departure from Central, the 1725 Buxton, was to be withdrawn after Friday 3. That weekend also saw the end of the Paddington to Birkenhead service. I set aside Thursday and Friday for the Buxton and Saturday 4 for Chester to Shrewsbury, so on Wednesday 1 I covered the down *Belfast Boat*. While checking what engine we had (45134 – 10A), I was greeted by a Patricroft crew that I knew well and they immediately invited me on to the footplate – most unusual actually at Victoria! We were soon on our way but without a torch I was unable to log in the dark and I was on the wrong side to read the speedo, so I just relaxed and savoured the experience of watching an experienced crew working an express passenger train with steam – all the way to Preston! Here, the fireman enquired after my plans and when I told him that I would have to 'suffer' a DMU back, the crew offered me another footplate on their return working – the Wyre Dock to Moston freight with 48553 (9H)! This was a bumpy but invigorating ride, and when we reached Brindle Heath the driver slowed down to drop me off by a convenient gap in the fence – what a memorable evening!

Next evening (2 March) I travelled to Buxton on the 1725 with 45150 (9E) and was planning to repeat the journey next day but I heard on the grapevine that 45562/93 were active at Holbeck, so I made a brief visit to Central to pay my last respects to 45150 and the Buxton before dashing over to Exchange to catch the 1734 (FO) to Leeds behind 44854 (55A). Yes, the Jubilees were working but *Alberta* was on the Bradford to Carlisle Fish and *Kolhapur*, the 2001 all stations to Skipton! I savoured a quiet Jubilee roar to Keighley with 45593, then to Forster Square for 42138 (55f) on the 2130 to Leeds City. I caught the overnight mails back to Manchester and there 73159 (9H) was heading the 0100 Glasgow, but I decided to go to Piccadilly for the 0117 to Cleethorpes,

From Winter into Spring 1967

worked to Guide Bridge by 45239 (9E), and, feeling weary, I then headed home.

Waking after 8 a.m., I dashed to Victoria where 70003 (12A) had just arrived on the 0720 Blackpool North, and I then endured forty miles of DMU to reach Chester. I began on the 1145 from Birkenhead with Caprotti 73139 (9H) to Chester, where 45116 took over to Shrewsbury but there was no repeat of this engine's heroics a month earlier, so I alighted at Wrexham and returned with 45042 (6A) on the 1225 from Shrewsbury. I then had a grandstand view of Clun Castle on the *Zulu* special before returning to Birkenhead behind another Patricroft Caprotti 73141 (Chester shed must have been short of locos for this last weekend). Later, 73097 (9H) headed the 1435 to Shrewsbury but I had to return to Manchester and work – my brief farewell to a wonderful train service was over.

The gloom of the following week was relieved by the 1705 Victoria to Blackpool North reverting to steam, worked by locos from a variety of depots. On Monday 6 I travelled to Poulton with 45435 (10A) and on the eighth, to Preston with 44909 (10F). Early on Saturday 11, I noted 42079 (9E) at Piccadilly on the 0117 before crossing to Victoria and the stock of the 0425 to York, worked by 44854 (55A). Near Todmorden, we crossed 44736 (9D) on the 0438 Halifax to Victoria and at Normanton the black five came off to be replaced by 77002 (50A)! I relaxed as we rolled along the Vale of York in the morning sunlight – casually observing the activity at the country stations on the journey. From York I headed to Leeds and caught 42093 (55F) on the 1015 to Bradford (Forster Square), returned with 42055 (56F) on the 1100 from Exchange and finally 42196 (56F) on the 1224 Wakefield to Bradford before heading for work.

Easter was approaching and the good news was that there were many steam-hauled reliefs, but the bad was that I had

From Winter into Spring 1967

to work lates every day. On Thursday 23, Patricroft's standard fives were out in force on North Wales extras. I went to Chester on the 1035 Bangor with 73097 (still in fine fettle); and was followed by 73144 (1214 to Llandudno), 73140 (1505 Llandudno) and 73073 on the 1620 to Llandudno. When this train was running, the Club regulars travelled on it and the 1630 DMU was virtually empty! On Good Friday, I headed in the opposite direction behind 73011 on the 0943 to Newcastle (banked by 73035) and returned from Leeds with the same engine on the 1214 relief. After work, I noted 44990 (56F) on the 2338 Liverpool to Leeds and 44732 (8F) on the 0100 Glasgow; Patricroft must have finally exhausted its standard five stockpile! On Sunday 26, 73144 worked the 2338, 73073 the 0100 and 44767 (12A) the 0110 Exchange to Barrow parcels.

On Easter Monday, the 1010 Victoria to Blackpool extra was routed via Hilton House and with ten on had to be double-headed by 45394 (10A) and 45101 (9D). I took it to Preston, where 45593 passed through on 1X15 Bradford to Blackpool North, and returned home with 44809 (8L) on the 0825 Glasgow.

At last, I now had two days off (twenty-eighth and twenty-ninth) but promptly overslept on the first morning. I dashed to Victoria just in time to see (and hear) 73096 and 73160 pound through on the 0930 Exchange to Newcastle relief so I had to make for Preston But at Leyland 44825 (12A) stormed past on the 0835 Barrow to Crewe! At Preston, 70005 headed south on the Carlisle to Crewe parcels – could it return on the 1537 Crewe to Glasgow? I waited for the 1100 from Windermere to Euston headed by 45450 (10D) and rode down to Crewe to investigate. 1530 at the north end of the station and no Britannia in sight but several Brush fours throbbing away, so I strolled back down the platform, wondering what to do next, when I heard an announcement of a Birmingham departure. Spotting that it was loco-hauled,

From Winter into Spring 1967

I suddenly made a seemingly illogical change of plan – instead of Glasgow, I'd head for Bournemouth!

I followed the usual NG route via New Street, DMU to Leamington and there picking up a through working to the southern region, but as I boarded this I walked straight into a posse of goldens conducting a census! I hurriedly detrained and waited for a DMU to Banbury, where I had to 'enjoy' the delights of the modern, plastic buffet for nearly two hours. I eventually reached Basingstoke in time for the 1815 Weymouth to Waterloo (34047), then down with 34090 on the 2235 to Eastleigh, 34056 0052 Eastleigh to Southampton, box back, then 34057 0230 Waterloo to Portsmouth and 34047 on the 0245 Waterloo to Bournemouth, on which I fell asleep. I woke with a jolt – we had stopped at Brockenhurst – so I took the opportunity of a last trip to Lymington, which was to be electrified from 2 April. I enjoyed 41320 on the 0704 down to the pier and back, where the Ivatt ran round the stock and formed the 0756 to Bournemouth. I reboarded and relaxed to savour this very late experience of an all-stations local on a main line.

On arrival, I retired to the local café for a much-needed hot breakfast and to study the timetable. I aimed to travel on a Southampton to Waterloo non-stop before returning north and the only possible train was the 0921 from Weymouth. This was sheer fate, as I knew nothing of the planning that had been involved with the working on this day!

I returned to the station for the 0924 to Waterloo, hauled by 35028, which slowly made its way to Southampton, touching 66.5 near Lyndhurst Road before two signal stops ensured a late arrival. The following up train was the 0940 Poole to Newcastle headed by 34004 – this was tempting but I resolved to stick to my plan – thank goodness. I went to the down side buffet for a coffee and my thoughts turned to the absence of southern enthusiasts. Where were they all? I soon had an answer, for, as I walked along the up platform, I could see that the end was a solid mass of DAAs who quickly advised, instructed, even ordered me to get on the 0921,

From Winter into Spring 1967

which by a miracle I had already planned to do. The train rolled in – the loco was 34089 (apparently, the last Pacific through works and in fine condition) and the driver was Ruben Hendicott of Nine Elms. The first coach was wedged on the mile post side so I grabbed a seat on the other side – my excuse for missing MP31! With ten coaches, 335.5 tons, we accelerated to 55 at Swaythling before a signal check at the airport and a signal stop for over 2 minutes shortly after. 34089 then pounded through Eastleigh and reached 69 after Winchester before repeated signal checks on the climb to Roundwood – we must have caught up with the Newcastle. From each check the loco showed terrific acceleration, so rapid that I could have believed that we only had a light weight load, and the driver whistled furiously, demanding a clear road. Finally, after Worting Junction, he got it. We tore through Basingstoke at over 80 and touched 95 after Winchfield, 88 at Farnborough and then 93 at Brookwood. 34089 and her crew had averaged 89.5 mph from Basingstoke to Brookwood! Severe signal checks at Byfleet brought us back to reality but we had experienced a Bullied light Pacific at its finest. I returned at a more sedate pace behind 35013 on the 1330 to Weymouth before starting the long, weary journey home but I will never forget my flying visit to Bournemouth!

34089 ten on 335.5 tons
0921 Weymouth to Waterloo (29 March 1967)

Miles				
–	Basingstoke	pass	0000	80/86
5.5	Hook	✓	0350	90/92
8	Winchfield	✓	0525	92/95
11.5	Fleet	✓	0734	92
14.75	Farnborough	✓	0939	88
20	Brookwood	✓	1312	93
23.5	Woking	pass	1556	

The Last Summer Saturday

Looking back from today, 1967 seems like Shangri La but at the time it felt as if the roof was falling in. Steam in Scotland had ended on 1 May, the Southern had gone out in a blaze of glory with Porter on the 0245 and I had what proved to be my last Jubilee over Ais Gill on 12 August behind *Alberta* on the 1017, returning south over Shap behind 45038 on the Glasgow to Blackpool North.

On Saturday, 26 August, I again tried for a Jubilee over Ais Gill but fate was to deal me a cruel blow. I headed for Leeds on the 0825 Manchester to Scarborough behind 45198 (8F), banked by 44891 (9D) to Miles Platting, and approaching City station I caught sight of 45562 waiting for its train to arrive. The Jubilee was very clean, blowing-off and certainly looked impressive to me, though some of the southern DAAs did query its ability to perform! When the stock arrived, the first coach was already wedged and by the time we reached Skipton it was jammed so I hastily changed plans and decided to return to Leeds and try for *Kolhapur* on the relief *Thames – Clyde*. I caught the 1035 from Morecambe with 45219 (55A) back to City station and then headed for Whitehall Junction. There were two ways of boarding, either by the road over-bridge, which was heavily 'gripped', or through the shed-yard and along the side of the track to the junction. With a band of fellow enthusiasts, I took this route but by the time we reached the lineside 45593 was preparing to depart, so we made a hectic dash towards the train. I had only run a short distance when I felt a stabbing pain in my chest, on the left side. I sat down on a low wall, assuming that it was a heart attack, but was much later to be informed that it was actually a spontaneous pneumothorax – the muscles between my lung and ribcage had torn open and every time I moved my ribs were digging into my lung. As 45593 stormed past me, I had a perfect close-up view of the immaculate Jubilee rounding the curve with the sun in a perfect position, but I was in too much pain to take the master shot! I staggered back towards the station, discovering that by holding my left arm close to my body the pain was less severe, so I caught a DMU to Wakefield and returned to Manchester behind 73025 (9H) on the 1335 from Scarborough.

When I reached Victoria, 44727 (12A) had arrived on the 1125 from Glasgow, followed by 44861 (9D) on the 1435 from Barrow – unusual, had the Carnforth five failed that morning? My chest pain was now easier, so I headed for Blackpool (by DMU – ugh!) and south of Preston I caught sight of 70039 on the Liverpool portion of the 1400 from Glasgow, followed by 44736 (9D) on the Manchester section. I carried on to North station and returned to Preston behind 45445 (10A) on the 1955 to Crewe. Here, I met the DAAs off *Kolhapur* (which had missed the tight connection at Carlisle into the 1400) and I was quizzed as to my failure at Whitehall Junction, so I invented a lame excuse, too proud to admit the real reason. We then boarded the 2048 to Blackpool with Pig 43029 (10D) and we relaxed while discussing the day's travels – my contribution was, 'It's not every day that you miss *two* Jubilees over Ais Gill!'

The next day, Sunday, I worked all day (despite the pain), but finished in time to catch the 2055 to Heysham, headed by 45390 (10A), to Bolton and return on the last 2015 from Blackpool North – a short-dated train which was part of a complex Kingmoor diagram, the loco working south on the previous days Glasgow to Blackpool North. However, for the last working it was Carnforth's 45209 in charge – and yet another steam working had ended.

The coming week was the last of the summer timetable and there wasn't time to cover everything, but one of my priori-

The Last Summer Saturday

ties was to make a last steam trip to Windermere. I chose Thursday, 31 August and began the day on the 0100 Manchester Exchange, worked to Wigan by 73160 (9H), reaching Heysham in time for the up *Belfast Boat Express* hauled by 45017 (10A) to Morecambe, where 44709 (10A) took over with one of Carnforth's keenest drivers, Tommy Owens, at the regulator. Regrettably, I have mislaid my logs for the period, but I can still remember his rapid starts and dramatic stops to this day. I travelled to Chorley, then returned to Preston in time for the 0815 to Windermere headed by 45436 which had recently been allocated to Lostock Hall from Birkenhead. This was a journey to savour, so I relaxed in a corner seat, admired the scenery and wished that this way of travel could last for ever – then I woke up to reality! At Windermere, I took photographs as the black five turned and then backed down on to its stock which now formed the 1100 to Euston. I was due to start work at 2 p.m., so I had to catch the 1217 Preston to Manchester (0825 Glasgow), which was actually a minus three-minute connection at Preston but 45436 ran to time and the Glasgow was behind us from Lancaster, so I could relax and then have 45350 (8F) on the 1217, noting that 43029 was waiting to work the 1244 to Blackpool South.

Next day, Friday 1 September, I finished work at 1 p.m. and dashed to Victoria for the 1327 to Glasgow. 44658 (8F) had already arrived on the 0825 from Glasgow and I boarded the 1327, headed by Newton Heath's 44893 to Preston where 70045 (12A), which had brought in the Liverpool portion, worked the combined train on to Carlisle. In previous years, this had been a Bank Hall Jubilee working and they usually took a pilot (2-6-4 Tank) from Oxenholme to Shap Summit but the Britannia worked on to Tebay before stopping for assistance and 75037 (12E) then banked the train to the summit. It is worth recalling that on 2 September 1966, 45055 (8K) with eleven on had worked right through unassisted – speed dropping to 18.5 mph at Shap Summit!

The Last Summer Saturday

After arrival at Carlisle, I headed for Kingmoor and was able to tour the shed. The highlights were 45562 and no fewer than twenty-three Britannias! In the gathering gloom it was difficult to judge exactly which were in traffic but for the record they were: 70003 (c) /5/6 (c), 70010/12/15(c)/16, 70022/23/25, 70031/33(c)/35/37(c)/38, 70040(c)/42(c)/45/46(c)/47/48(c) and 70051/52(c). ((c)= condemned).

I returned to the station and savoured a meal in the staff canteen before the long wait for the 0222 to Crewe, which was headed by yet another Brit – 70014. I must admit that I don't recall much of this journey as I slept through most of it, but from Crewe I returned north for the 0800 Carlisle to Birmingham. At Preston, 44893 (9D) was heading a Bury to Blackpool North excursion and 70032 (yet another one) was working the 0810 Barrow to Euston. I then caught the 0800 Carlisle behind 70035 down to Warrington and returned north with 44933 (8A) on the 1134 Crewe to Blackpool south. We crossed 44971 (10D) on the 1055 Blackpool North to Crewe and I glimpsed 70004 on Springs Branch shed – I had seen twenty-six Britannias in less than twenty-four hours!

At Preston, 45411 (9D) arrived on the 1327 from Manchester and I then slumped on to a platform bench, exhausted, but still able to savour the atmosphere of the swan song of steam on the West Coast Line. Then, 44917 (10D) rolled in on the 1055 Euston to Barrow, running early (on an easy schedule), much to the disgust of the southern loggers on board who had been used to much better performance than this! The final highlight was the passage of the 1532 Crewe to Carlisle (non-stop) headed by 70025, but a waiting DAA needed this loco to complete the class for haulage so he clambered aboard as it crawled through the station!

Unfortunately, he was spotted by a station inspector who ordered the train to be stopped and searched! No doubt more 'neverers' piled on board in the confusion but I had to return to Manchester on the 1435 Barrow behind 44709 (10A) to work a late turn – for me, the last summer of mainline steam was over.

45435 at Morecambe Promenade with the 0730 to Manchester Victoria (BBE) Sunday, 28 April 1968 – a reminder of those cool, damp mornings as enthusiasts savour the atmosphere before departure.

The Belfast Boat Express (BBE)

Although the *BBE* was steam-hauled until 5 May 1968, it had been officially dieselised on 21 July 1962 but thanks to those 'wonderful' Metro-Vicks it soon reverted to more reliable motive-power – black fives! The train was not a regular feature of my travels until September 1967 as the up journey arriving in Manchester at 8 a.m. and the down departing in the evening at 2055 just did not fit in with either my working hours or other steam diagrams.

Until 18 April 1966, the 1607 – Barrow and the 1722 – Windermere (Crewe diagrams – either Britannias or ex-works locos) were my usual targets after an early turn, and when these trains were withdrawn we still had the 1705 – Blackpool North and the 1710 to Southport until 6 January 1967 when 44891 (1705) and 44845 (1710) headed the last official workings, though the Blackpool was worked by 70004 on 30 March and by 45203 from 7 to 12 April 1967.

After this, I concentrated more on the *BBE* and realised that the best way to cover the up working was to go overnight, leaving Manchester on the 0100 Glasgow (usually a Patricroft standard five to Wigan), then the Barrow sleepers to Lancaster and after a walk to the bus station boarding a workmen's bus to Heysham (old faithful number 87). 31 August 1967 was typical – 73160 (9H) on the 0100, 45017 on the 0615 Heysham to Morecambe where 44709 took over to Manchester Victoria.

The full weekday diagram for the loco was: 0630 Morecambe to Manchester Victoria, 0915 Parcels Manchester Victoria to Blackpool North via Oldham and Bury, 1345 return parcels and finally the 2055 (SX), 2105 (SO) Manchester Victoria to Morecambe. On summer Saturdays, the engine and stock worked the 0927 Manchester Victoria to Barrow and 1435 return instead of the parcels. In the early

The Belfast Boat Express (BBE)

Sixties, the locomotive was provided by Newton Heath, usually a black five though Jubilees did appear, even as late as Saturday, 1 May 1965 when 45600 powered the 2105, but after Sunday, 3 October 1965 when 45271 (9D) worked the duty, Lancaster shed took over (usually 44889 or 44758) until 18 April 1966 when the shed closed and Carnforth supplied the loco. From this date, their Top Link crews worked the 0630 up to Manchester and the parcels back to Preston except on Sundays when a Newton Heath crew took over at Preston. The down train was worked by Patricroft men to Preston (Monday to Friday) – Lostock Hall (Sat and Sunday) – where a Carnforth crew took over. The Patricroft crew returned on a Wyre Dock to Moston freight.

After the end of the 1967 summer timetable, I regularly travelled on the 2055 to either Bolton or Preston, having to return by DMU – even on a Sunday as the 2015 Blackpool North to Manchester Victoria (worked by the Kingmoor five off the Saturday 1105 Glasgow) had ended on 27 August, thus denying a steam return from Bolton. Carnforth was rostering its best black fives to the duty and three engines in particular became regulars – 45017, 45025 and 45342 – and the regular crews were to become equally familiar.

On 15 November 1967, I travelled out on the 2055 behind 45390 right through to Heysham, spending the night on the station (never again!) and returned on the 0547 (45054) to Morecambe where 45390 took over for the run back to Manchester. I watched the engine take the ECS to Red Bank and hastened to the buffet for much-needed refreshment. About 9 a.m. I walked over to Platform Seventeen bay where 45390 was hooking on to the stock of the 0915 parcels. The driver asked me if I was working today and when I replied, 'Not till 4 p.m.' he invited me on to the footplate for the trip back to Preston! The route to Bolton was unusual, via Oldham, Rochdale and Bury, track almost impossible to cover by steam at that time. At Preston, I thanked the

The Belfast Boat Express (BBE)

friendly crew and waited for the 0825 from Glasgow and after the Type 4 had left with the Liverpool portion, 45048 (8F) worked the Manchester portion and on arrival at Victoria I had completed over 200 miles of steam haulage. After work, I headed for Exchange and caught the 0100 Glasgow worked to Wigan by 73132, then on to Lancaster and bus to Morecambe for a much-needed breakfast in Barry's Promenade Café. I then dashed to the station for the 0630 and the loco had changed to 45017 for the journey to Manchester. On arrival, I hung around the seventeen bay and this time the guard asked me to join him in the brake for a Spartan ride to Preston, where I again waited for 1217 which was unusually worked by a Britannia (70051). By this time most of the remaining Pacifics were diagrammed to work the heavier parcels and freights and the remaining passenger workings were class fives!

Into December, and on the afternoon of the twentieth the *BBE* loco failed at Patricroft and the foreman had no hesitation in replacing it with the near ex-works 73134 which had been overhauled at Cowlairs in July 1965 (after which, I was amazingly pulled by it on the Heads of Ayr branch!) and on return was put into store from August 1965 till November 1967 – fuelling rumours of the strategic reserve.

The start from Platform Twelve at Victoria is both curved and graded and 73134 took over 3 minutes to pass Salford, then accelerated to 56.5 at Agecroft, easing to 55.5 through Clifton Junction, then reached 56.5 on the 1 in 200 at MP6, 54.5 at Kearsley and 55.5 through Farnworth – well up to the best black five performance. After a 25 mph signal check at Burnden we arrived in Bolton in 16 minutes 55 seconds (about 15–45 nett). The run on to Chorley had just about everything in it – slight slips on the curve from Bolton and a signal check to 30 at Lostock Junction meant that we dropped over 2 minutes to Horwich Fork but the driver then let the engine have its head: 72 at Blackrod, 82 at Adlington and still 77 round Adlington Junction (smooth riding) before

The Belfast Boat Express (BBE)

easing right down to a crawl and dropping another minute on to Chorley! The overall time was 16 minutes but from Horwich Fork to Adlington Junction was 2 minutes 20 seconds – the fastest that I have ever recorded on any train. The run on to Preston was standard (ugh) with 73 after Farington Junction and on alighting I observed a somewhat bemused Carnforth crew taking over before I had to return home for an early start next morning.

The next day (twenty-first) 45287 (8A) was on the diagram, so I went to Leeds behind 45034 (8C) on an additional 1747, but next day 73134 was again on the *BBE*, so I booked a bed and breakfast in Lancaster. Unfortunately, the 2055 left 15 minutes late due to extra holiday traffic and, having lost its path, suffered a signal check to 5 mph at Windsor number two, and then a dead stand at Windsor Bridge number three. From the restart, we reached 51.5 at Clifton Junction, dropped to 49.5 at MP6 before reaching 53 at Kearsley. We left Bolton 13 minutes late and 73134 and her driver gave us a fine run to Chorley – 54.5 over Horwich fork and 68.5 through Adlington, giving a time of 14 minutes 12 seconds, my second best. On to Preston, we suffered three more signal checks and left for Lancaster over 8 minutes late. The Carnforth crew made a careful start with their strange steed, dropping nearly a minute to Oxheys (against the best black fives) but they then demonstrated that 73134 could run by maintaining 75 mph from Garstang to Oubeck (76.5 max at Galgate) reaching Lancaster in 22 minutes 37 seconds gaining 1.5 minutes on schedule. I retired to the local bed and breakfast and next morning returned to Manchester behind 73134. We left 8 minutes late and with subdued running, that's how we stayed, but the two down runs had shown that the standard Caprotti fives could climb as well as the black fives and were capable of rapid acceleration.

Late December 1967 saw the last Pacific workings – 70024 on the 0730 Exchange to Leeds (twenty-fourth), 70012 worked

The Belfast Boat Express (BBE)

the 0150 Exchange to Barrow parcels (twenty-seventh) and later that day 70013 arrived on the 0805 Carlisle to Red Bank, later to work the last 1747 (FO) to York on the twenty-ninth. Unfortunately I was working, so my last Britannia was 70021 heading the 1217 Preston to Victoria on the twenty-eighth.

Into 1968, and the *BBE* was still steam and I was to spend much of the next four months travelling on it. On Sunday, 21 January I went down on the 2055 behind 45390 and next morning at Morecambe Promenade I was surprised to see 44848, a Rose Grove engine, on the 0630 up. I was just about to say to the driver that he had an unusual engine when, after a quick look down the platform, he opened the cab door and nodded for me to climb on to the footplate! I stayed there for the whole journey and 44848 and her crew were to give an exhilarating performance. After a brisk start from Lancaster, we reached 62.5 at Galgate, 70 at Bay Horse, 80 at Garstang and, still accelerating, 82 at Brock before a distant double-yellow thwarted the drivers attempt at 90 mph with a black five (a feat he *was* to achieve in the very last week of steam). After a further check at Green Bank, we reached Preston in 22 minutes 42 seconds (possibly 22 minutes nett). The run to Chorley was marred by a signal stop at Euxton but on to Bolton we reached 62 at Horwich Fork summit before a check at Bullfield. The fine running continued from Bolton with 66.5 at Kearsley, and 68.5 past Agecroft Junction reaching Salford in 12 minutes 4 seconds – just beating my best time by 3 seconds! I travelled back to Preston in the parcels brake and finally returned to Manchester with 44809 on the 1217 – what a wonderful morning!

The next highlight was the evening of Friday, 2 February when Driver Barton of Patricroft with 45017 recorded a time of 14 minutes 8 seconds to Bolton. The start was electric, passing Salford in 2 minutes 12 seconds and solid running (55.5 at Kearsley) meant we were approaching Bolton 3 minutes early and we amazingly had a completely unchecked run into the platform!

45435 at Platform Sixteen, Manchester Victoria, after arrival with the 0730 from Morecambe (BBE). Sunday, 28 April 1968.

44888 waits for the end at Stockport Edgeley, 4 May 1968. The shed closed the following day.

The Belfast Boat Express (BBE)

By now the 0100 Glasgow was rostered diesel but Patricroft's Caprotti fives were appearing, and on 21 March I travelled to Wigan with 73135 and then on to Heysham. From there, 45390 worked the *BBE* to Morecambe where 45025 took over, one of its now regular appearances. On the twenty-sixth and twenty-ninth 45212 (10D) worked the 2055 but the end was now in sight with the news that the diagram was to be dieselised from Monday, 6 May.

Into April, and on Saturday 13, 73134 was working the 0100 to Wigan so I decided to go overnight to Heysham, where 44758 worked the *BBE* to Morecambe and 44894 took over to Manchester. This was Easter weekend and surely there wouldn't be any steam-hauled reliefs? Amazingly there was one – 45268 on a Blackpool to Colne extra which I joined at Preston in the evening of Monday 15. We left at 1930 but at Accrington the sharp-eyed station inspector realised that much of the train was empty and wanted to terminate the relief there! This caused a near riot in the enthusiast-crowded first coach – we had been promised that this train was going to Colne and we demanded that it should. Eventually, the inspector relented and we were on our way to our destination. I caught a DMU back to Manchester but several DAAs remained in the ECS for the return journey. Unfortunately the loco was derailed whilst turning at Rose Grove!

45025 was now the regular *BBE* loco and on Sunday, 21 April it had a ten coach load (333 tons nett) but was handicapped by the severe 20 mph PWS at Agecroft which was to mar the final two weeks. We fared better from Bolton, topping Horwich Fork at 42.5 mph but after Chorley we had two signal stops. Between Preston and Lancaster another severe PWS to 25 mph had been imposed (was this deliberate?) at Brock, but we then reached 63 at Oubeck with this heavy load. I returned on the Monday morning with 45025 and the

The Belfast Boat Express (BBE)

usual seven coaches and on arrival in Manchester I noticed that the 2325 Glasgow had not arrived. It eventually rolled in at 0950 (over 3 hours late) behind 73069, which meant I was able to photograph its arrival in sunlight. The 1217 Preston was now only steam on Mondays so I returned to Preston and had 45330 (now at 9D) back – I noted 44942 on the 1244 to Blackpool south.

Into the final weeks and 45025 worked the *BBE* continuously from 17 to 26 April, and on 23 to 25 April Driver Ernie Harrison was on the up working and Driver Ted Fothergill on the down – what a combination! However on Friday 26, Driver Morby took over the train at Preston and I logged my fastest time to Lancaster (on the Heysham). After a fine start, we passed Oxheys in just over 3 minutes and then steady acceleration gave 73.5 at Garstang and despite a signal check outside the station we stopped at Lancaster in 22 minutes 19 seconds (22 minutes nett). On the next day Carnforth shed provided heap-of-the-year 45394 (sick joke?) for Harrison but he got 72 out of it before the Barton PWS. Thankfully, on Sunday 28 he had 45435, which touched 82 at Brock before the PWS. The Bay Horse to Brock time was under 6 minutes.

The final week arrived with a further threat – BR planned to ban steam haulage of *all* passenger trains from 6 May, so on Monday 29 I went out to Preston to return with 45268 (9D) on the 1217 and this indeed was the last time that the working was steam. One plus was that the 0100 was worked by standard fives for most of the week – 73128 (30 April), 73050 (2 May) and 73157 (Friday 3), which encouraged me to go overnight to Heysham on all three nights. I was day-off on this last date and I decided to cover as much of the diagram as possible. We had 44709 on the 0615 from Heysham where 45342 took over with the wonderful crew of Driver Ted Fothergill and his regular fireman Dave Marsden. Unfortunately, leaving Lancaster, Ted had to make an

The Belfast Boat Express (BBE)

emergency stop but from this he accelerated to reach 78.5 after Garstang before braking for the chronic Barton PWS. The best section of the run was from Chorley to Bolton, when 45342 maintained a steady 62 from Blackrod to the summit and reached Bolton in 14 minutes 49 seconds, my best time. We then rocketed out of Trinity Street, passing Moses Gate in 2 minutes 50 seconds to a max of 66 at Keasley Junction before the Agecroft PWS but despite this we reached Salford in 12 minutes 53 seconds (possibly 11.5 minutes nett). At Victoria I retired to the buffet for refreshment before crossing to Platform Seventeen, where 45342 was taking water. Ted asked me if I was working later and when I said no he invited me on to the footplate for the circuitous journey to Preston. I really savoured this ride, watching a Top Link crew in action and admiring the varied scenery of the Oldham loop and the Rochdale to Bury line. All too soon we reached Preston, and I thanked the crew for inviting me to join them on this memorable day. I then caught the 1244 to Blackpool South (44816) where I considered a dash to North station for the return parcels, but I decided against it, returning by DMU (ugh).

I waited at the south end of Platform Six and soon 45342 rolled in with its vans and a friendly crew waving to me – but feeling dog-tired and with the brake van and familiar guard in front of me, I opted for the 'comfort' of the van! On arrival in Manchester I bade the guard and crew a fond farewell and, looking back, the warmth and generosity of the last steam crews was understandable as they faced an uncertain future. Only the enthusiasts showed any interest in their work and expressed sympathy for their position – even the formerly dreaded shed foremen were now offering us cups of tea!

After a leisurely meal in the Silver Pool, I returned to the station and 45342 was preparing to leave on the 2055. We made a fast start to Salford (2 minutes 27 seconds), then eased for the Agecroft PWS, then 48.5 at Farnworth before a severe signal check at Burnden meant we actually took over

The Belfast Boat Express (BBE)

17 minutes to Bolton – probably 15.5 minutes nett. The running on to Preston was the finest I had ever experienced and we stormed through Loston Junction at 55.5 in less then 5 minutes, 58 over the summit and a max of 72 through Adlington Junction gave a time of 13 minutes 28 seconds to Chorley. The pace continued as we rounded Euxton Junction in 4 minutes 49 seconds, then 72 after Farington and a clear run in gave a time of 11 minutes 36 seconds to Preston, beating my previous best by over a minute! On to Lancaster with Driver Jones of Carnforth and, after the Barton PWS, he accelerated to 76.5 at Galgate. I alighted, exhausted but exhilarated after a truly wonderful day and headed for the bed and breakfast and a very good night's sleep.

Saturday morning, 4 May, awake at 6 a.m., a quick breakfast and a dash to the station. 45342 arrived on Platform Five (unusual) and Ted Fothergill was at the regulator – a senior driver working his last express passenger train with steam. We respected his privacy and boarded the first coach and, on leaving, the five slipped several times (damp rail?) but Ted soon regained control and accelerated rapidly, reaching 82 at Brock before severe braking for the hated Barton PWS. The time to passing Brock was 14 minutes 36 seconds, only 4 seconds slower than my fastest – Driver Owens with 45017 in 1967 (after a rocket start!). On from Preston, the performance was magnificent – 57.5 at Leyland and 47.5 at MP 23.75 where the safety valves lifted! The time to Chorley (11 minutes 46 seconds) was a record for me and the run on to Bolton was almost a repeat of the previous day – just 18 seconds longer. From Bolton, the same high standard was maintained and despite the severe PWS at Agecroft, Driver Fothergill and his able fireman stopped in Salford one minute early – a fitting tribute to the fine work of the Carnforth crews and their black fives over the preceding years.

Elsewhere, events were grim as the Liverpool and Stockport sheds were closing that weekend and I had time for a last visit to Heaton Mersey and Edgeley, where 44781

The Belfast Boat Express (BBE)

arrived on shed just as I was about to leave and with 44871 rostered for the last working (2331 to Leeds) – two engines that were famously to meet again – I took farewell photographs before heading for work after two memorable days.

I woke early on Sunday morning – the sun shone – so I walked to Agecroft Junction where I photographed 45025 on the last up *BBE* as it 'drifted' by. On to Victoria for another shot as the ECS pulled out and then 44871 and 45269 passed through being reallocated from Edgeley to Bolton.

All that remained was the last down working and 45025 gave a solid performance – 53 at Farnworth, and Bolton to Chorley in 14 minutes 56 seconds. I alighted at Lancaster and watched as 45025 and the *BBE* headed into history, before walking to the bed and breakfast knowing that life would never be the same again.

45025 passing Agecroft Junction with the last up Belfast Boat Express – Sunday, 5 May 1968.

73069 passes through Manchester Victoria heading for Red Bank with the EVS of the Wigan parcels. 11 June 1968.

*The End of Manchester Steam*_____

After the dieselisation of the *Belfast Boat* on Monday, 6 May 1968 and the BR steam ban, Manchester had no booked steam passenger departures – but still two early morning arrivals, 0545 from Wigan (2335 Glasgow) – a Patricroft five and the 0210 from York – a Newton Heath five. However, by mid-week there was a strong rumour that one last departure was being arranged. The date was Saturday, 11 May, and the train the legendary 0100 Exchange to Glasgow.

On the Friday I was conveniently working a late turn, so midnight found me walking across the city centre to Exchange. I had made the journey many times in the previous three years, but tonight I had mixed emotions – looking forward to a steam overnight (albeit a short one), but realising that this was almost certainly the last. I walked along Platform One, past the familiar rake of sleeping cars, vans and compartment stock to the loco – 73133, very appropriate as a representative of the type (Caprotti standard five) which had for so long been associated with Patricroft shed and this train. I joined fellow enthusiasts in the first coach and we were soon on our way. In years gone by there would have been a hectic exchange of news of the previous day's workings and plans for the rest of this day, but by May 1968 there wasn't a lot to discuss, so the atmosphere was quiet and subdued.

On arrival at Wigan we alighted immediately – no point staying on-board for the shunt, the station pilot was now diesel – and headed for the down side waiting room with its famous graffiti-covered walls telling of engines seen, trains missed and long, long waits! We had decided against a fill-in trip to Preston to keep the overnight 100 per cent steam and instead chose to savour the delights of North Western

93

The End of Manchester Steam

station for four hours! Our wait was broken by the arrival of 45055 on the 0125 parcels from Manchester, which would then work the 0550 return. We settled down in the waiting room and talk turned to the highlights of the last year, leading to a suggestion that if there were awards, what would they be? A friend and I developed the idea and we eventually formed our own personal proposals for The Last Year of Steam Awards (up North of course). They were:

Driver	Ted Fothergill (10A)
Fireman	Jacky Harrison (26A)
Footplate	Tim's Northwich to Workington (on an 8F)
Log	45017 Manchester Vic to Bolton: 14 m 8 s (2/2/68)
Thrash	45116 from Gobowen (4/2/67)
Wedge	1017 Leeds to Carlisle (26/8/67)
Lurch	73014 at Clifton Junction (72 round 50 limit)
Station	Hebden Bridge c/o 0210 York to 0420 Manchester Vic)
Ticket	Millow to Ansdell OR
Bus	Morecambe & Heysham's No 87
Chippie	Edge Hill
Café	Barry's (Morecambe Promenade)
Chinkie	Silver Pool (Manchester Vic)
Diesel	Metro-Vicks (innumerable failures)
Footbridge	Bolton (many a close shave)
Subway	Liverpool Exchange (off 0859 for 0900)
Cart	0859 arrival Liv ex (for 0900)
Riot	2250 York to Manchester Exchange missed connection with 0100 (all aboard the 0105 parcels!)
Mass grip	Dumfries (off 1017 Leeds)
Eff	Blackpool North off 45565
Froth	0900 Manchester Victoria to Glasgow (no heat so 44780 requisitioned) 10/12/67
Gripper	(from a very long list) Tom Punk (so human), Tache (cunning), or Killer (ruthless)
Neverer	Leeds
DAA	TBA. We must have a vote before it's too late!

Eventually the Glasgow rolled in. We changed platforms, watched 45055 back on to the rear portion and then relaxed for a gentle return to Manchester (easy schedule with recovery time). In mileage, this steam overnight could not compare with those of the past to Aberdeen or Bournemouth – but it was my last.

The following weekend (18 May) the last 0332 Leeds/0210 York to Manchester was worked by 45310 and on the twentieth 73069 arrived at Exchange on the last steam 2335 Glasgow. I now had to concentrate on freight and parcels, and on Friday, 24 May the 1912 empty stock was worked by the ultra-rare 44777 (a long-time Cricklewood resident), which had been transferred to Patricroft when Edge Hill closed. I needed this five for haulage so I approached the friendly driver who gave me a footplate from Victoria number 11 to Exchange Platform One with the 0100 ECS, my last new black five (the 478th!).

Into June, and the long hours of daylight gave more scope for photography. A favourite scenic location was Heap Bridge, east of Bury, where a succession of eastbound evening freights crossed the viaduct and began the climb to Broadfield. The sunny evening of 12 June was typical with 48692 (9K) on the 1805 Burnden to Moston, 45350 (10F) the 1905 Burnley to Moston, 45394 (10A) on the late running 1650 Heysham to Moston and finally 45209 (10A) the 2020 Bolton to Bedford Parcels.

I tried for the Crumpsall coal train (7 June) on the very steep gradient into the station but overslept and missed 45318 (9K) which had just arrived! I moved on to Summerseat Viaduct and was rewarded by 45290 (9k) on the Bury to Ramsbottom coal train.

Another target was Chequerbent on the subsidence-steepened climb from Atherton (Bag Lane) but on the 10 June the main working was diesel (banked by 48374 (9H)). I tried again on the thirteenth, but only a two-wagon load for 48491 (9H).

73069 Leaves Eccles Yard with the 1020 Stott Lane to Mold Junction. Monday, 24 June 1968.

48773 climbs away from Bury with the MRTS Rail Tour, 28 July 1968.

Patricroft's finest (in 1968), 73134 and 73069, pound through Greenfield with the SVRT. 20 April 1968.

Plenty of steam in Victoria – but it's the final week! 48620 (Banked by 45055) heads for Miles Platting with the 1330 Windsor Bridge to Brewery, as 45206 recovers from assisting 48319 earlier. 25 June 1968.

48319 and 45206 start the climb to Miles Platting as 44884 shunts a failed DMU. Tuesday, 25 June 1968.

45290 crossing Summerset Viaduct, 7 June 1968, with the Bury Ramsbottom Coal.

45394 at Heap Bridge, 12 June 1968, on the 1650 Heysham to Moston Freight.

45394 passes Horwich Fork Junction with the 1650 Heysham to Moston, 10 June 1968.

44781 passes through Manchester Victoria with Trip 214, 25 June 1968.

45287 leaves Preston with the 1005 Ribble Sidings to Heysham while 44874 shunts the Maudland Coal. Friday 2 August, 1968.

The End of Manchester Steam

The Saturday afternoon Colne to Red Bank Vans was still steam – 45350 (10F) on the fifteenth at Blackburn and 45096 (10F) on the twenty-second, which I photographed passing Agecroft Junction – my last picture here, where I had spent many hours train-spotting in my youth.

Dawn, Monday, 24 June 1968, and I stood on the footbridge overlooking Patricroft shed yard as steam was being raised for the last week of operation. In years gone by, there would have been at least sixty locos being prepared for service but on this last Monday morning there were only nine. They were:

45055	0435	Exchange Pilot
45156	0545	Moston
48491	0615	Mottram
48775	0652	Moston Atherton
48170	1000	Ship canal
73069	1020	Stott Lane – Mold Junction
73050	1912	Empty Vans – exchange
73133	2225	Warrington
73125	2315	Edge Hill

45287 was banking at Exchange and was later to work the 1820 to Oldham Road. My gloomy mood was deepened by the sight of 73134 on the condemned line – only twelve years old and in near ex-works condition. My thoughts flashed back to its spirited running on the *BBE* in December 1967 and, in August 1965, when ex-works it turned up at Heads of Ayr!

I was working late turns all week, so I could only take morning photos and the obvious engine to aim for was 73069 which was in clean condition after working the Two Cities Rail Tour the previous day. After breakfast in a local café, I strolled along to the footbridge on the eastern side of Eccles station where years before I had watched Scots tear through on Liverpool to Newcastle expresses.

106

As I climbed the steps, I turned to see that 73069 and its train had already arrived in the yard and was ready to depart. I took up my position and at 1125 the standard five whistled and began its journey to Chester. I took two approach shots, then rushed to the top of the stairs for a going-away picture which included the four-track layout through Eccles station.

I then headed for Kearsley, but due to a guards' dispute all three freights that I hoped to see were cancelled and the three locos passed light engine.

On Tuesday 25 I overslept and didn't make Victoria till nearly midday, only two hours before starting work. Should I try for the Agecroft to Dewsnap on Hunts Bank, I wondered, was it running and could I get back in time? The weather was gloomy so I decided not to take the risk – but at 1220, 48319 rolled through and stopped on the bank for 45206 to buffer up and they then stormed up to Miles Platting and I could only take a going-away shot from the end of the platform. Then at 1350 I was just about to leave when whistling from Exchange heralded the approach of the 1330 Windsor Bridge to Brewery headed by 48620 and banked by 45055 and I could only take a platform picture as they stormed by – I think I made the wrong decision!

On Wednesday I had to work, but a close friend made contact – he had arranged access to an empty cotton mill overlooking the (former) junction of the Newton Heath to Oldham line with the now lifted Werneth incline. At dawn on Thursday we climbed to the top floor – a panoramic view but very overcast skies. At 8 a.m. 48620 climbed to Werneth with a short freight before my pal had to leave for work. I was left alone in the eerie silence of the empty mill and waited and waited till 1125, when 44735 climbed the bank with the 1027 Victoria to Oldham parcels. By now I was cold and hungry and about to give up when I heard the noise of two steam engines working hard. 48773 came into view on the 1130 Brewery to Royton Junction – a lengthy freight

The End of Manchester Steam

banked by 45268, an impressive sight and sound but the light was still poor. Would the sun ever shine for this last week? Looking back, the answer was no! I was later informed that 45156 was rostered for the next day's 0255 Exchange to Bangor Parcels – should I try for a footplate or maybe the guard's van? But at midnight I was exhausted after a very long day, so I had to head home for some sleep.

Friday, 28 June 1968, the last day of steam banking to Miles Platting and I had to try for the 1045 Agecroft to Dewsnap. I arrived on Hunts Bank at 1110, just in time to miss the late running 1027 Oldham parcels but at midday I could see two columns of steam and smoke leaving Victoria – the Dewsnap was starting the climb! That was the good news – the bad was that the train engine, 45290, is tender-first but the banker 44735 was working very hard – the driver saw me and stuck his arm out of the cab to give me the thumbs up – storming past just a few feet away. The ground truly shook as I returned the spirited driver's greeting to thank him for the endearing memory of steam in Manchester.

Saturday 29 was a total anti-climax – Patricroft had only 45055 working as Exchange pilot, Newton Heath had 44809, 45206/68 and 45310/30 in steam to be reallocated, and Bolton rostered 45269 for the Dewsnap but it was cancelled – a sad end to working steam in Manchester.

44735 pounds up Hunts Bank, banking 45290 on the 1045 Agecroft to Dewsnap. Friday, 28 June 1968 – the last day of steam banking to Miles Platting.

44735 climbs out of Preston with the Darwen to Heysham oil tanks, 4 July 1968.

The End of Steam

After the shock of no more Manchester steam and being physically drained by three years of continuous steam bashing, I spent the next few days just eating, sleeping and working, but by Thursday, 4 July I had recovered sufficiently to begin recording the final month. After finishing an early turn, I caught a DMU to Preston, visited Lostock Hall shed and then photographed 44874 near Farington on the 1505 Heysham to Warrington vans. I returned to the station just as the sun broke through and taking a position in the old shed yard, I was rewarded at 1950 with the wonderful sight and sound of former Newton Heath favourite 44735 pounding north with the Darwen to Heysham oil tanks – and the sun still shone!

The following evening I concentrated on the Wyre Dock coal workings and caught 48400 at Bamber Bridge on the 1435 to Burnley before moving to Farington Curve Junction for several shots of a steamy 48765 on the 1840 Rubble sidings to Rose Grove – with the friendly crew well-posed at the cabside in the evening sunlight.

The next week I had Wednesday and Thursday off, so I booked two nights bed and breakfast in Carnforth. I arrived at Lancaster in the early afternoon of Wednesday 10 and walked up to number one bridge to photograph 44874 on the 1505 from Heysham before moving on to Carnforth and booking into my lodgings. The evening was partially sunny so I headed for Arnside Viaduct, but the sun had slipped behind thin cloud in the west when 44897 came across with the 2028 Barrow to Preston Mails at 2105. There was still enough light for a silhouette with the exhaust visible along the length of the train – an evocative sight.

The End of Steam

Thursday dawned dull and wet but the good news at the station was that 45268 had left on the 0755 to Windermere after a DMU failure. A generous enthusiast gave me a lift north to an over-bridge where we photographed the five returning with three LMS corridors, and racing back to Carnforth station I was able to board for the next stage of the diagram to Morecambe. The engine and stock then worked the 1115 to Lancaster and the 1150 return so I enjoyed the rest of the morning in the comfort of an LMS compartment behind a black five on local service – what a pleasant surprise!

In the afternoon, I returned to Lancaster number one to photograph 45388 on the 1430 Heysham to Ribble Sidings and 45231 with the 1505 Heysham to Warrington before another trip to Arnside to view an unidentified five cross in poor light with the mails.

The following week, a close friend invited me to join him for a day's photography in East Lancashire – including Copy Pit. I readily accepted for, even though I lived only thirty miles away, I had never actually been there! We chose Wednesday, 17 July and arrived near the summit just after 7 a.m. but overcast skies and the first freight being diesel-hauled was disheartening. We took up position for the 0653 Farington to Healey Mills and at 0810, 48773 stormed over the top. We then drove down to Rose Grove to find out what was working and from there targeted 48340 on the 1050 Burnley to Wyre Dock. Heading for Rishton, we took up a position just west of the station and photographed the 8F and its mixed freight framed by the trackside bushes in full bloom – a very pleasing sight.

Returning to Rose Grove, we found 48393 ready to depart eastbound on a train of bogie-flats, so we raced the short distance to Cliviger Woods for a scenic setting – very nice too!

After a break, we concentrated on 48062 working the 1905 Burnley to Moston, obtaining shots at Rose Grove, Rishton, Lower Darwen and Bradley Fold before returning home – a long day, but well worth the effort.

45388 prepares to depart from Blackburn with the 1914 Colne to Preston Vans, Tuesday, 23 July 1968.

44971 leaves Skew Bridge with the 1835 Ribble Sidings to Warrington, 19 July 1968.

44971 leaves Preston and heads into the setting sun with the 2050 to Blackpool South, 8 June 1968.

48730 climbs Farington Curve with the 1640 Wyre Dock to Rose Grove, 22 July 1968.

A black five drifts down through Rishton with the 1840 Ribble Sidings to Healey Mills, 17 July 1968.

The Rishton bushes will bloom again, but the 8Fs will soon be gone for ever. 48340 heads the 1050 Burnley to Wyre Dock Coal, 17 July 1968.

48773 near Copy Pit summit with the 0653 Farington to Healey Mills (I didn't have time to remove the bushes!), 17 July 1968.

48393 climbs through the scenic Cliviger Gorge with what we thought was the 1045 Wyre Dock to Healey Mills. 17 July 1968

The End of Steam

The next evening (Thursday, 18 July), we drove to Houghton and were rewarded with the sight of 44781 working very hard on the 1 in 100, heading the 1840 Ribble Sidings to Healey Mills, followed by 48666 with the 1640 Wyre Dock to Healey Mills. Moving on to Preston station, we noted 45206 on the 2028 Barrow, 45388 with the 1914 Colne Mails and 44888 heating the sleepers.

I returned the following evening as the overnight (FO) Manchester Victoria to Yarmouth was conveying a Preston portion for the start of the local holidays – and it was booked steam! I watched 44971 leave on the 1835 to Warrington freight, 45212 worked the 1850 Ribble sidings to Carnforth, 45388 on the 1914 Colne and, unusually, 73069 arrived with the 2028 Barrow Mails. Finally, a very clean 44781 rolled in with the stock of the Yarmouth portion and it was a delight to return home to Manchester behind steam, instead of the hated DMUs! I had travelled this road over a hundred times with steam haulage and this was to be my last – fittingly with a familiar loco that had been allocated to Agecroft for nearly twenty years, up to the sheds closure in October, 1966.

The next day (Saturday 20) was clear and sunny but I had to work till late afternoon before dashing to Preston for the two evening passenger workings. I arrived to be informed that 45388 was working the 2050 to Blackpool and 45212 the 2125 Liverpool. So, after meeting an old friend, we decided to try for a shot of 45388, which was in clean condition, on Kirkham curve. At 9 p.m., the sun was still shining, but unfortunately the train was running 15 minutes late and pounded round the curve just after the sun had set! Looked good – but could have been perfect.

Sunday 21 dawned clear and sunny, so I decided to follow the RVR Tour – but without road transport I was restricted in locations. I began by photographing 44888 west of Patricroft station, then on to Crows Nest for 70013 rounding the curve away from the junction and I managed to catch the Pacific again passing Burscough Junction station. Finally, I returned to Manchester for a long-distance picture of 45110 passing Cornbook carriage-sidings, going away towards Central – and the sun shone all day.

Next day, Monday 22, I reached Preston in the late afternoon and got a lineside close-up of clean 45017 heading the 1505 Heysham to Warrington. I then moved to Farington Curve for 48730 on the 1640 Wyre Dock to Rose Grove.

The following day (the twenty-third), I spent a few hours at Lancaster noting 45073 on the 1005 Ribble Sidings to Heysham, 44874 with the following 1150, and 44817 powering up to number one on the 1505 Heysham to Warrington. Later in the day I reached Blackburn in time for 45388 standing in the evening sun with the 1914 Colne to Preston parcels.

On Friday 26, I spent a few hours at scenic Rishton and photographed several 8Fs on the Wyre Dock coal trains and 45212 heading the late running 1050 Ribble to Rose Grove, but I was then caught hopelessly out of position by the surprise appearance of 45073 on an up ECS!

On Saturday I was working a long late but managed a morning trip to Preston for the 0958 Barrow parcels worked by the still-clean 45025.

Sunday was again sunny and I followed the MRTS Tour – walking up to the Boars Head from Wigan I was rewarded with 70013 working very hard on the climb then over to Chorley for 45073 and 45156 crossing the viaduct and eventually reaching the old gas-works junction on the climb from Bury with 48773 pounding westward – a very scenic sight.

The End of Steam

My thoughts were now focussed on the final weekend (2 to 4 August) when I was rostered to work every day – but by a combination of swapping days off with work colleagues, calling in favours due, even a little financial persuasion, I was finally able to get the three days off.

Friday 2 dawned clear and sunny and I caught an early DMU to Chorley. My target was the 0730 Farington trip on the 1 in 131 at Rylands so I walked there in the warm sunshine. I took up position and waited, and waited, until at 0915 45318 emerged from the tunnel with its short freight. The loco was very clean, the scene perfect – apart from a PW inspector who appeared from nowhere and stood by the lineside – right in line with the engine! I had to take the picture and then turned to get a close-up going-away shot – lovely.

I moved on to Preston and the over-bridge north of the station and at 1100 got 45287 on the 1005 Ribble to Heysham (3T41) including empty cattle wagons (and plenty of clag), followed by 44874 on the Longridge trip. I then retired to a local café for lunch during which I noticed that I was near to the end of a roll of film – black and white, which I had always used. The sun was still shining, so I decided to change to colour – I wasn't going to get another chance!

Later in the afternoon I headed for Rishton and while strolling round the station the signalman called me over to his box and invited me in! He made tea and we talked about the past, the sun shone and the view was superb – heaven (if only it hadn't been the eve of Armageddon!).

At 1920 his bell rang – the 1905 Burnley to Moston (extended to Partington) was leaving Accrington. I took up position on the footbridge and 48167 pounded through, hauling a long train of loaded coal wagons – the ground shook! I returned to the box for more tea and chat until the bell rang again – the last 1914 Colne to Preston vans was on its way. I dashed round to the lake but the light was fading as 45407 crossed at 2005. I then enquired about the 1840 Ribble Sidings to Healey Mills but it was running over an

The End of Steam

hour late, so I bade farewell to the friendly signalman and caught a DMU to Blackburn. As we passed through the tunnel on the approach I could see the 1840 just entering and 48423 pounded past – the crew illuminated by the firebox glow – a wonderful vignette of footplate action! 45407 was ready to leave for Preston so I dashed towards the engine to be met by a very famous DAA rushing in the opposite direction, shouting, 'The footplate's wedged – lets try the brake!' By now, the guard was on the platform waving the right-away so with cries of, 'We're official photographers for Railway —' we jumped aboard. Desperate, but it worked. We savoured the journey (62 max at Pleasington) and on arrival we thanked the guard and my last sighting of the day was 44781 rolling in on the 2028 Barrow Mail.

Dawn at Carnforth on Saturday, 4 August 1968, as for the last time a steam shed prepared for a day's work. The sky was heavily overcast so my colour pictures were going to be way underexposed. 45342 set out for Barrow at 0620, 44735 for Heysham and 75019 moved off shed and, later, into history. A quick visit to Arnside but the café was wedged, then to Morecambe for 45390 on the 0925 Lancaster to Heysham parcels and on to Lancaster where the sun came out! 45231 passed through with the Sandside to Farington ballast and 44709 arrived with the Kendal trip. I met a fellow DAA on the platform and he confirmed that 75019 had returned to Heysham, so the 1455 to Carnforth (6P52) must be running! We set out for the wilds of Heysham Moss and by a combination of a bus journey and a long walk we arrived at Sandside before 1500. The cloud had returned, but after a short wait we heard the sound of a steam engine working hard and 75019 rounded the distant curve and headed towards us with a very long freight. We had time to take several pictures before the last steam-hauled freight on BR disappeared into the distance.

We then headed south for Preston and the wonderful news that not only 45212 was working the 2050 to Blackpool

The End of Steam

South, but that 45318 was working the 2125 to Liverpool Exchange. By 8 p.m. the station was crowded with enthusiasts and banks of photographers – the travelling public must have wondered what on earth was happening. I watched 45212 depart and then waited for the 1725 Glasgow to arrive. As it stopped, I jumped aboard the first coach of the Liverpool portion – but it was already jammed. The Manchester portion departed and 45318 backed on – the whole station was illuminated by hundreds of flash-bulbs! I managed to stand by a window and we departed to more flashes of light. After negotiating Farington Curve, 45318 accelerated to 66 at Rufford, dropped to 59 at Ormskirk and then reached a max of 78.5 at Maghull, arriving in Liverpool at 2159 – an era had ended.

48765 threads Farington Curve Junction with the 1840 Ribble Sidings to Rose Grove. Friday, 5 July 1968.

On the day before it went into the history books, 45318 approaches Chorley with the 0730 Farington trip. Friday, 2 August 1968.

After sunset, 44897 crosses Arnside Viaduct with the 2028 Barrow to Preston mail, 10 July 1968.

'Thunder in the Peak'. 44949 and 45110 pound up to Chapel with the Severn Valley Rail Tour, 20 April 1968

44874/45017 climb Hunts Bank with the second returning SLS tour. Sunday, 4 August 1968.

The Very End of Steam

On Sunday, 4 August 1968, friends drove up early from London and we set out to photograph the rail tours that were criss-crossing Lancashire. We went to Greenfield first for the two SLS specials (double-headed black fives) then on to Entwistle Viaduct for the LCGB (44781/70013), the SLS tours, and the RCTS with 48476 and 73069. Amazingly the sun shone all day from a cloudless sky!

My friends had to return south in the late afternoon and, after they had dropped me off on the climb to Miles Platting I photographed the first returning SLS (1Z78) with 44871/94 working hard on the 1 in 59 of Hunts Bank in a low evening sun. That was my last colour frame, so I had to rapidly reload with black and white and cross to the opposite side of the line in time for 44874/45017 with the second SLS (1Z79).

A fellow enthusiast gave me a lift back to Victoria where I caught a DMU to Moses Gate for 45156 returning with the GC Enterprises tour and, though the light was fading, I took a picture with the now redundant Bolton Loco Coaling Plant in the background. I returned to Manchester and waited for the LCGB tour (1L50) which was running very late.

I stood at the eastern end of Platform Thirteen when 70013 rolled in, a carriage door opened right in front of me and, without thought, I climbed aboard. *Oliver Cromwell* was soon on his way and for the last time I savoured the sound of a steam engine working hard up to Miles Platting, twelve coaches and a box. On reaching Stockport Edgeley, crowds thronged round the Pacific singing, 'So long, it's been good to know you', as I made my way to the opposite platform for the return home. Later, as I reached Victoria Bus Station, I heard the plaintive cry of a chime-whistle in the night air – 70013 was returning to Lostock Hall.

The Very End of Steam

All that remained was the 'fifteen guinea special' on Sunday 11, when a close friend and I planned to just potter around South Lancashire taking a few photographs. We began by the trackside near Glazebury and 45110 was being worked quite hard as it passed by, and then on to Kearsley – not another photographer in sight! The weather was clear and sunny as, in the distance, 70013 climbed the bank, a magnificent sight but what was that dark patch on the front of the boiler? I looked into the sky and, amazingly, a small cloud was casting a shadow on to the engine and it was moving at the same speed and direction! I delayed as long as possible...

The weather was now perfect; we looked at one another – Ais Gill? Why not. When we reached Ribblehead all the best positions were wedged, so I took a shot of the Britannia from the shaded side – came out quite well. After lunch in Hawes we headed for the summit but the narrow road was blocked by hundreds of parked cars, so we had to leave ours and walk. I was looking for a decent position on Mallerstang when the two black fives came up, almost noiselessly, playing with their load, so I had to take a long-distance cross-shot with the line of parked cars as a back-drop! We raced back south for a final, fleeting glance of 45110 crossing Earlestown Viaduct and mainline steam had ended where it began – both historically and for me personally – between Manchester and Liverpool.

- And so to those magnificent locos like 45025, 45342 and 73134,

- to those enthusiastic fireman like Jacky Harrison, Dave Marsden and John Carter,

- and to those wonderful drivers like Ernie Harrison, Jacky Barton and dear, old Ted Fothergill – thanks for the memory.